Biblical Hebrew with Joy!

Introduction to Hebrew Grammar using the Holy Scriptures

Joy Carroll

Biblical Hebrew with Joy!

Introduction to Hebrew Grammar using the Holy Scriptures

2021 by SimkhaPress
ISBN: 978-1-7333230-3-1

The websites and phone applications cited in this book were active at time of publishing. There is no guarantee that they will continue to be available in the future.

For free Video Series, PowerPoints and Audios for use with this book, visit: HebrewWithJoy.com

Biblical Hebrew with Joy! may be purchased at special quantity discounts. For more information, visit HebrewWithJoy,com or contact Joy at hebrewwithjoy33@gmail.com

Published 12-27-21
Revision 10-13-24

Dedications

Biblical Hebrew with Joy! (BHJ) is dedicated to Esh Gray, Pam Neilson, Deb Wiley and Erin Miskey. You never stopped encouraging me to write this book!

Todah Rabah (thanks very much) to:
BHJ Prayer Team: Your faithfulness to pray for me through this project provided the encouragement, inspiration, strength and energy to complete BHJ.
Graphic Designer: our wonderful daughter, Becca Kendall
BHJ Editing Team:
Erin Miskey, Rachel Zoller, Deb Wiley, Pam Neilson, Jackie Newman, Heather Martin, Michelle Bonville, Sandy Pham, Juliet Abrego, Kwai Ying Den, Mariya Schoening, Natasha Cinkosky, Patti Gasper, Paul Sung, Ruth Sung, Rhonda Devorah Brown, Sabrina Johnson,
Proofing: Erin Miskey, Rachel Zoller
Author Photo: Randie Ide

A very special thanks to our congregations, Etz Khayim and Kol Dodi, for supporting and encouraging my Hebrew classes over the years.

Todah rabah (thanks so much) to all of my Hebrew students, who, for many years, have encouraged me to continue teaching and writing.

Testimonials

Biblical Hebrew with Joy! is an incredible addition to Joy's first book *Hebrew with Joy!* and her second book *Hebrew with Joy! in the Biblical Feasts*. Never before has Hebrew been taught in such a creative and thoughtful way. Every word, every example, and every challenge is truly inspired.

Joy's deep desire to share her love of the Nation of Israel (*Am Israel*), the culture of the people, and the deep spiritual appreciation of her Jewish heritage simply pours out on every page. Her commitment to teaching Adonai's holy language in a way that is easy, inspiring, and more importantly life changing, is clearly a calling on her life.

Her personal journey has led her to embrace her Jewish roots in a way that flows like a spring from her soul to share with the rest of us.

Thank you, Joy, for this treasure of a teaching series! May it be a blessing to all who learn from it.

- Pam Neilson, Meveseret Zion, Israel

Learning the beautiful language of God will sustain and strengthen a person's heart. *Biblical Hebrew with Joy!* left me in awe of God, even more!

- Juliet Abrego, Colorado

Reading Scriptures without its original tongue is incomplete; a piece of beautiful jigsaw puzzle lost in translation. *Biblical Hebrew with Joy!* is that part 2 which breathes the Alef-Bet into Life... a must have accompaniment to *Hebrew with Joy!*

- Kwai Ying Den, Colorado

Table of Contents

Introduction

Shalom and welcome to ***Biblical Hebrew with Joy!*** **(BHJ)**

The *Hebrew with Joy!* series is designed for beginners who have a desire to learn Hebrew, the Holy Language of the Living God. The first book in the series, *Hebrew with Joy!*, focuses on the Hebrew Alef Bet (alphabet) and should be completed before moving on to this book.

For additional Hebrew reading practice and vocabulary building, you may want to complete *Hebrew with Joy! in the Biblical Feasts* before studying this book.

Because of the amount of information in each lesson, many teachers and students have found that it is helpful to spend two class sessions on each lesson. As a result, there are two videos for each lesson.

Video Lesson Files are a part of the learning system and are available at no charge. They allow you to study on your own – almost like being right in the classroom! These lessons can be helpful whether teaching individuals, families, home school, Bible study or other groups. The videos are available to download at hebrewwithjoy.com/BHJ-videos password: BHJvideos

Audio files are so helpful if you are an audio learner. The files are available at no charge and can be accessed on our website: hebrewwithjoy.com/BHJ-audios

Handouts (which include flashcards) can be downloaded and printed at: hebrewwithjoy.com/BHJ-handouts

Technology: In this book, you will be introduced to many computer and phone applications (apps). If technology is NOT your favorite thing, please make sure you have a Hebrew-English Interlinear Bible available and a Strong's Concordance.

Pronunciation: *Biblical Hebrew with Joy!* teaches the *Sephardic* form of pronunciation to honor the standard pronunciation used in Israel.

Scripture References: Occasionally, you will see Scripture references that look like this: Psalm 19:1(2) This means that in some Bible versions, the Scripture is in Psalm 19:1 (NIV, NASB, NKJV) and in other versions, the Scripture is in Psalm 19:2 (TLV, CJB)

Suggestions for Students:

- Try to study with a partner or in a group. The accountability and interaction will aid in learning.
- Practice using the flashcards to learn the new vocabulary and grammar (Appendix F).
- Try *not* to write the Hebrew transliterations (English sounds) above the Hebrew in the book! This will slow down the learning process.
- After each lesson is taught, use the learning activity that goes with the lesson. It will reinforce the materials in a fun, up-beat way.
- Listen to the audio files between class sessions to reinforce the new vocabulary as you practice your pronunciation.
- Have fun as you learn the language of God!

Suggestions for Teachers:

- Be sure that the students know the Alef-Bet before taking this class. If needed, suggest that they complete the *Hebrew with Joy!* book first.
- Encourage students to use the flashcards (Appendix F) to reinforce the new vocabulary and grammar.
- Try to discourage students from writing the Hebrew transliterations (English sounds) above the Hebrew in the book! This will slow down the learning process.
- Allow students to work as partners as much as possible. For example, partners can practice reading and translating with each other before speaking out loud to the entire class.
- Be sure to call on all students to read out loud.
- When a student is reading out loud and makes a mistake, *first* ask the student to try the word again. Then, if they still struggle, ask if another student can help. As a *last* resort, the teacher pronounces the word.
- After each lesson is taught, use the learning activity that goes with the lesson. It will reinforce the materials in a fun, up-beat way.
- Encourage students to listen to the audio files between class sessions. This will especially help the auditory learners.
- Video Lessons can also be used as a teaching tool. The files are available to download at hebrewwithjoy.com/BHJ-videos

Lesson 1 - Alef-Bet and Roots

A – Introduction & Review

Shalom שָׁלוֹם students! So glad you have joined me for *Biblical Hebrew with Joy!* May this book draw you closer to Adonai, our wonderful LORD, as you study His Holy language! A1

Why did I write this book when there are so many Biblical Hebrew books available? My main motivation was to provide a user-friendly, easy, and joyful way to learn that would appeal to students of any age. In addition, I wanted to include special Scriptural and Israeli "treasures" that would draw the readers deeper in their love for Adonai, His land, and His people.

This book has two main goals: First, to study Biblical Hebrew words, roots and grammar, making Bible study richer and more meaningful. Second, to encourage students to write their own Hebrew prayers to Adonai. This goal requires a certain amount of modern Hebrew understanding, as our English sentence structure is more like modern Hebrew. So, *Biblical Hebrew with Joy!* is a blend: it focuses mainly on Biblical Hebrew but does include a limited amount of modern Hebrew.

Please Note: This course is designed to be used **AFTER** you have completed the introductory course, *Hebrew with Joy!* **or** if you have a solid knowledge of all Hebrew letters and vowels. In this lesson, you will be able to do a "self-check" to see if you are ready to move on in this book or if you should complete *Hebrew with Joy!* before continuing.

English Transliterations and Accented Syllables are based on the following: A2

a	"a" as in all	kh	"ch" as in Bach
e	"e" as in egg	ay	"ay" as is lay
ee	"ee" as in feet	ai	"i" as in pie
o	"o" as in over	oy	"oy" as in boy
oo	"oo" as in too	ooey	"ooey" as in gooey

CAPITAL letters show the accented syllable in a word as in "*sha-LOM*"
If the accent is *not* on the last syllable, it will be **BOLD** as in "***ME**-lekh*"

Review Quiz

Are you ready to move into *Biblical Hebrew with Joy!?* To find out, take the following self-check to test your Hebrew knowledge. Write the number of the English sound that matches the Hebrew letter/s. (The review quiz continues on the next page.) <u>Please don't use any resources to complete this quiz.</u>

A4

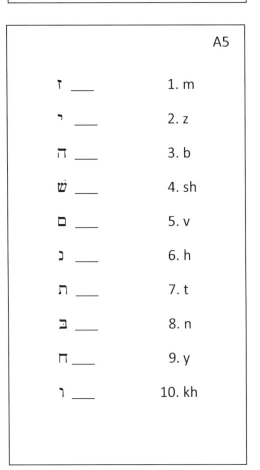

ע ___	1. d
צ ___	2. r
פּ ___	3. silent
ר ___	4. s
ק ___	5. k
ד ___	6. ts
ס ___	7. p

A3

א 3	1. m
ג ___	2. f
פ ___	3. silent
שׂ ___	4. l
כ ___	5. g
מ ___	6. s
ל ___	7. kh

A6

Numbers can be used more than once!

תַ___	1. too
תוֹ___	2. tee
תִ___	3. tie
תוּ___	4. tah
תַי___	5. toe
תֵי___	6. teh
תֵ___	7. tay
תִי___	8. tooey
תֶ___	9. toy
תוֹי___	
תוּי___	

A5

ז ___	1. m
י ___	2. z
ה ___	3. b
שׁ ___	4. sh
ם ___	5. v
נ ___	6. h
ת ___	7. t
ב ___	8. n
ח ___	9. y
ו ___	10. kh

Match the words: A8

קָדוֹשׁ___	1. joy
שִׂמְחָה ___	2. Sabbath
שְׁמַע ___	3. hear, listen
שָׁלוֹם ___	4. life
אַהֲבָה ___	5. instruction
בָּרוּךְ ___	6. blessed
תּוֹרָה ___	7. love
שַׁבָּת ___	8. holy
חַיִּים ___	9. peace,hello,goodbye
יְהוָה ___	10. name
שֵׁם___	11. LORD

Match the roots: A7

שׁ.ב.ת ___	1. live
שׁ.מ.ע ___	2. joyful
א.ה.ב ___	3. hear and obey
ק.ד.שׁ ___	4. holy
י.ר.ה ___	5. rest, stop
ב.ר.ך ___	6. hit the mark
ח.י.ה ___	7. love
שׁ.ל.ם ___	8. bless, kneel
שׂ.מ.ח ___	9. completion, wholeness

Please check the quiz answers below. A9

A3	4,1,7,6,2,5,3 ←from top
A4	4,1,5,2,7,6,3 ←from top
A5	5,10,3,7,8,1,4,6,9,2 ←from top
A6	8,9,6,2,6,7,3,1,2,5,4 ←from top
A7	2,9,1,8,6,4,7,3,5 ←from top
A8	10,11,4,2,5,6,7,9,3,1,8 ←from top

***If you were able to complete 80% of the answers correctly,
you are ready to move on in *Biblical Hebrew with Joy!*
If you were not able to answer 80% correctly, please review *Hebrew with Joy!*

B – Overview Pre-Quiz

This pre-quiz will show you how much of the new course content from this book you already know. It is also great overview of what is covered in this course. Don't worry if you don't know the answers now! By the end of the course, the Hebrew will be much more familiar. <u>Please don't use any resources to complete this page.</u> B1

Match the roots to their meaning: B3			
guard ,keep	_____	ש.מ.ר	A
remember	_____	צ.ו.ה	B
command, order	_____	ד.ב.ר	C
create, shape	_____	ב.ר.א	D
give	_____	נ.ת.ן	E
grace, mercy, favor	_____	ז.כ.ר	F
speak, word, thing	_____	ע.ב.ד	G
work, serve, worship	_____	ח.נ.ן	H

Match the pronouns to their meaning: B2			
I	_____	אַתְּ	A
you (fs)	_____	הֵן	B
they (mpl)	_____	הִיא	C
you (ms)	_____	אֲנַחְנוּ	D
they (fpl)	_____	אֲנִי	E
he	_____	הֵם	F
she	_____	הוּא	G
we	_____	אַתָּה	H

Match the prefixes to their meaning: B5			
to, for	_____	מ..	A
from	_____	בְּ..	B
in the, with the	_____	ו..	C
the	_____	ל..	D
and	_____	הַ..	E
in, with	_____	בַּ..	F

Match the suffixes to their meaning: B4			
my, me	_____	..נוּ	A
your, you	_____	..ךָ	B
his, him	_____	..וֹ	C
our, we	_____	..◌ִי	D

Translate the sentences into English:		
	הוּא נוֹתֵן לְךָ.	B6
	אַתָּה אֱלֹהֵינוּ!	B7
	אֲנַחְנוּ אוֹהֲבִים אֶת מִצְוֹתָיו.	B8
	בָּרוּךְ בְּנֵי יִשְׂרָאֵל.	B9

Answers are at the bottom of Appendix A, page 119.

C – Roots

From the root of one tree, come many similar branches, each different and unique. C1
Hebrew roots are the same! From each root, come many words that share similar meanings.

<table>
<tr><td rowspan="2">Root meaning:
bless, kneel</td><td rowspan="2">ב.ר.ך
Used 330X in the Scriptures!</td><td>Most roots are built from three letters.</td><td>C2</td></tr>
<tr><td>Middle and bottom dots and vowels are not written in roots.
(Note: In this book, periods are used between the letters of the root.)</td><td>C3</td></tr>
<tr><td></td><td>בָּרוּךְ</td><td rowspan="5">Words from the same root share similar meanings. Vowels, prefixes and suffixes change the meaning.</td><td rowspan="5">C4</td></tr>
<tr><td>knee</td><td>בֶּרֶךְ</td></tr>
<tr><td>will bless you</td><td>יְבָרֶכְךָ</td></tr>
<tr><td>blessing</td><td>בְּרָכָה</td></tr>
<tr><td>blessings</td><td>בְּרָכוֹת</td></tr>
</table>

Fill in the missing English word above. (The Fill-In answers are in Appendix A, page 119.) C5
In the Hebrew words above, circle the root letters meaning to "bless" or "kneel."

A complete list of the roots included in this book is in Appendix E, page 125. C6

D – Reading Scripture

The Scripture below is the first phrase in the beloved Aaronic (Priestly) blessing which is found in Numbers 6:23-27. We will study the entire blessing in a future lesson. Circle the root letters meaning "bless/kneel": D1

יְבָרֶכְךָ יְהוָה וְיִשְׁמְרֶךָ׃

The LORD will bless you and keep you...

Complete the English translation below. Then, write the Scripture in English from your favorite translation. Finally, read the Scripture out loud in Hebrew and English. D2

יְהוָה.	בְּשֵׁם	הַבָּא	בָּרוּךְ	תְּהִלִּים 118:26
	in (the) ________	the one who comes		Psalm 118:26
				Normal English

Write the missing Hebrew word below. Then read the Scripture aloud two times and circle the root letters: D3

בָּרוּךְ אַתָּה ______________

Blessed are you, LORD! Psalm 119:12

D4

> **בָּרוּךְ אַתָּה יְהוָה...**
>
> *"Blessed are You, Adonai..."* These beloved words from Psalm 119:12 begin many Jewish prayers, a testimony to the reverence and devotion belonging to Adonai alone. Many of these prayers are included in the Feasts of the LORD called מוֹעֲדִים – appointment times with GOD.

E – Hebrew Phrases

Read the new Hebrew phrase below three times out loud: E1

Thank God! *(Blessed is the Name)* !בָּרוּךְ הַשֵּׁם

When a Jewish person hears a great report or victory, he/she responds with
!בָּרוּךְ הַשֵּׁם
Immediately, the credit goes to "haShem" – "the Name" given by the Jewish people to their mighty LORD. As we read in Psalm 18:50(49), "Therefore I praise You among the nations, Adonai, and sing praises to Your Name." (Tree of Life Version) E2

If you successfully completed this lesson, !מַזָּל טוֹב Mazal Tov! (Congratulations!) E3
Be sure to complete the learning game and the homework assignment on the following pages to reinforce what you have learned before moving to the next lesson.

As we go forward in *Biblical Hebrew with Joy!,* we can truly say
!בָּרוּךְ הַשֵּׁם (Thank GOD!) for his Holy Language of עִבְרִית (Hebrew.)
May this book draw you closer to Adonai, His land, and His people in amazing new ways!

F – Resources

Starting in Lesson 2, you will be introduced to Hebrew technology resources to help you go deeper in your Hebrew study. F1

<u>If you are more comfortable using books instead of your computer or cell phone, please make sure to have access to the following resources:</u>

Strong's Concordance .1 F2
Hebrew – English Bible (Interlinear is best) .2
Hebrew-English Dictionary .3

Scripture & Phrase Game

Cut out the Hebrew words below or download them from: **https://hebrewwithjoy.com/bhj-handouts/** Then, in groups or individually, use the words to create the four Scriptures or phrases from Lesson 1. When you are done, read all the Scriptures and phrases and try to translate them. (Variation: take a blank sheet of paper and number it 1-4. Then write the four Hebrew Scriptures/phrases on the paper.)

יְהוָה	אַתָּה	בָּרוּךְ
יְבָרֶכְךָ	הַבָּא	יְהוָה
בָּרוּךְ	בָּרוּךְ	בְּשֵׁם
וְיִשְׁמְרֶךָ	הַשֵּׁם	יְהוָה

Lesson 1 Homework

שֵׁם_______________

Write down and review any difficult letters, vowels, words or roots from the Review Quiz A3-A8: .1

Fill in the missing Hebrew words. (Don't forget the vowels!): .2

Hebrew	English
שָׁלוֹם	peace
	LORD
	blessed
	instruction
	name
	love

Fill in the missing English words: .3

Root Meaning	Root
holy	ק.ד.שׁ
	ח.י.ה
	שׁ.מ.ע
	שׁ.מ.ח
	י.ר.ה
	שׁ.ב.ת

Fill in the missing English and Hebrew words from the scripture below (Hint – check C2 in the lesson.): .4

	בְּשֵׁם	הַבָּא		תְּהִלִּים 118:26
LORD			blessed	
				normal English

Write <u>three</u> Hebrew words (and their English meanings) that come from the root ב.ר.ך: .5

_______________ _______________ _______________ English

_______________ _______________ _______________ Hebrew

Fill in Psalm 118:26 <u>twice</u> (on BOTH LINES) below in Hebrew. .6
Then, using the internet, listen to the song below:

Baruch Haba by Paul Wilbur

______ ______ ______ בָּרוּךְ

Blessed is He who comes

יְהוָה ______ ______ ______

Who comes in the name of the LORD

Now arise, oh LORD! Come to your resting place,
You and the ark of Your might
Then we will rejoice, as we're clothed with Your righteousness
And celebrate the love

Write your own Hebrew prayer to Adonai using the Hebrew phrases in this lesson to help .7
you. Use either block or script Hebrew letters. (See Appendix C and D, pages 122-124)
<u>For those of you who like to journal, start including simple Hebrew prayers and Scriptures every day!</u>

Translate your sentence prayer into English: .8

Memorize the new root and new words in this lesson. To help you, .9
listen to the audio files available on the *Hebrew with Joy!* website:
<u>https://hebrewwithjoy.com/bhj-audios/</u>
You can also print the flashcards in Appendix F, pages 127-136, or download the lesson flashcards from: <u>https://hebrewwithjoy.com/bhj-handouts/</u>

Lesson 2 - Pronunciation

Hebrew Prayer	
Thanks very much for...	תּוֹדָה רַבָּה עַל...

A – Vocabulary

Memorize the following Hebrew words used in this lesson:

English	Gender*	Transliteration	Hebrew	
all	-	*kol* *(exception vowel)*	כָּל	A1
bread	*ms*	***LE**-khem* *(exception accent)*	לֶחֶם	A2
king	*ms*	***ME**-lekh* *(exception accent)*	מֶלֶךְ	A3
GOD	*ms, mpl*	*el, e-lo-HEEM*	אֵל, אֱלֹהִים	A4
wisdom	*fs*	*khokh-MA* *(exception vowel)*	חָכְמָה	A5

**Gender: ms=masculine singular, fs=feminine singular mpl=masculine plural, fpl=feminine plural* A6

B – Hebrew Pronunciation

Examples		Origin	Accent	Name	
to-RA sha-BAT	תּוֹרָה שַׁבָּת	Israel, Middle East, Spain, Portugal, North Africa	Accent is usually on the ________ syllable.	**Sephardic**	B1
TO-ra **SHA**-bas	תּוֹרָה שַׁבָּת	France, Germany, Eastern Europe (origin of most Jewish Americans)	Accent is usually on the **FIRST** syllable.	**Ashkenazi**	B2

B3

Pronouncing Biblical Names

Israeli Hebrew teacher, Rivka Simms, shares this Hebrew tip: Almost all Hebrew names found in the Scriptures are accented on the last syllable. For example, Abraham אַבְרָהָם, Isaac יִצְחָק, Jacob יַעֲקֹב and Moses מֹשֶׁה.

C – Pronouncing יְהוָה

In this course, I have chosen to use the word "ADONAI" when pronouncing יְהוָה, the "unpronounceable name of G-d," used over 6000 times in the Scriptures! Feel free to use the name you are comfortable with. C1

D – Pronunciation Exceptions!

Occasionally, the "Kametz" vowel ָ has a long "o" sound as in "fl<u>o</u>w." D1

Examples: כָּל = kol חָכְמָה = khokh-MA

Read the following Hebrew words twice (using the exception vowel). Then, write the English translation below the Hebrew word: D2

חָכְמָה	הַכָּל	כָּל
________	everything	________

If the <u>last</u> syllable of a word is חַ, the sound is "akh," and the prior syllable is accented. D3

Examples: רוּחַ **ROO**-akh (wind/breath/spirit) נוֹחַ **NO**-akh (Noah)

If there are two "Segol" vowels ֶ ֶ side-by-side, the first one is accented. D4

Example: מֶלֶךְ **ME**-lekh

In the following Hebrew words, <u>circle the accented syllables</u>, then read the words aloud twice. Finally, write the missing English translation below the Hebrew words: D5

לֶחֶם	אֶרֶץ	רוּחַ	אֱמֶת	מֶלֶךְ
________	land	________	truth	________

D6

לֶחֶם

In Deuteronomy 8:3, Adonai tells us that "...man does not live by לֶחֶם alone but by every word that comes from the mouth of Adonai." Throughout the Scriptures, לֶחֶם represents "bread" or the staff or sustenance of life. The root of this word ל.ח.ם is also the root for "fight" (נִלְחַם) and "war" (מִלְחָמָה.) For centuries, Rabbis have debated the connection between these three words. Some Rabbis wrote that ancient wars were primarily fought over bread (economic sustenance). Others suggested that man first must sweat and struggle for his daily bread (Genesis 3:19) and then struggle with his fellow man to keep it.

(excerpt from *Worthy Brief* by George Whitten www.worthybrief.com.)

E – Shva Vowel ְ

The Shva ְ vowel can be challenging to pronounce. Sometimes it has a short sound "uh" (as in "upon") and sometimes it is silent. (A complete list of vowels is in Appendix D, page 124). The following chart will help you determine whether to "sound" the vowel or not: E1

Example	Silent or Sounded?	
שְׁמַע	**Beginning** of a word: Shva is always sounded	E2
יִשְׂרָאֵל מִשְׁפְּחוֹת נְרַנְּנָה לַבְּרִיאוֹת	**Middle** of a word: • Shva is usually silent and ends a syllable. • If there are 2 Shvas side by side, the first one is silent and the second one is sounded. • When a Shva is under a letter, and that letter is then repeated, the Shva is sounded. נְרַנְּנָה (joyful cry) • When there is a dagesh (dot in the middle of a letter), the Shva is sounded	E3
בָּרוּךְ	**End** of a word: Shva is always silent	E4

In the following Hebrew words, circle the SILENT Shvas, then read the words aloud twice. Finally, write the English translation below each Hebrew word: E5

עִבְרִית   חָכְמָה   יִשְׂרָאֵל   בְּשֵׁם   בָּרוּךְ

_______   _______   _______   in (the) name   _______

E6

עִבְרִית

What is the original meaning of עִבְרִית "Hebrew," the Holy language of GOD? We find that the root (ע.ב.ר) means to "cross over." Truly, ADONAI asks us to leave the idols in our lives behind and "cross-over" to worship Him alone. As we are reminded in Joshua 24:15:

If it seems bad to you to worship Adonai, then choose for yourselves today whom you will serve—whether the gods that your fathers worshipped that were beyond the River or the gods of the Amorites in whose land you are living. But as for me and my household, we will worship Adonai! (TLV)

F – Syllable Lines

A helpful way to pronounce a new word (especially a long word!) is to break it into syllables first, then pronounce each syllable: F1

מִ | תּוֹ | רָ | תֶ | ךָ

kha te ra to mee ←

Each syllable will have only ONE sounded vowel: F2

יִשְׂ | רָ | אֵל

el ra yees ←

If the Shva is silent, it does not count as a sounded vowel. F3
In the above example, notice the Shva under the Shin;
it is silent and ends the syllable.

In the following Hebrew words, draw syllable lines, then read the words aloud twice. Finally, write the missing English translations below the Hebrew words:

F4

מִתּוֹרָתֶךָ	וְיִשְׁמְרֶךָ	אֲהַבָה	יְבָרֶכְךָ	יִשְׂרָאֵל
from your instruction	and will keep you	______	will bless you	______

G – Cantillation Marks

The special markings in Biblical Hebrew are called **cantillation marks**. They are used to divide verses into smaller units of meaning and have musical value, allowing Cantors (song leaders) to chant the verses. These marks also show the accented syllable of each word. (*Notice the accent marks circled in the Scripture from Psalm 119:18 below.*) G1

גַּל־עֵינַי וְאַבִּיטָה נִפְלָאוֹת מִתּוֹרָתֶךָ׃ G2

from your instruction wonders and (I will) behold my eyes uncover

Memorizing Scripture

G3

One of my greatest blessings has been to memorize Scripture בְּעִבְרִית (in Hebrew!) During my quiet times, before reading the Word, I recite Psalm 119:18 (G2 above) out loud in Hebrew. Why is memorizing important? The answer is found in Psalm 119:11:
"I have treasured Your Word in my heart, so I might not sin against You."
To treasure Abba's Word in your heart in Hebrew is a treasure indeed!

H – Root ח.כ.ם

Words from the Root		Root Meaning	Root	
	חָכְמָה	to be wise	ח.כ.ם used 149X In the Scriptures	H1
wise	חָכָם			

In the Scripture below:

Fill in the missing Hebrew and English words. H2

Write the Scripture in normal English from your favorite translation. H3

Draw syllable lines. H4

Read the Scripture twice using the accent marks to help you pronounce it correctly. H5

חָכְמָה	יִתֵּן	יְהוָה	כִּי־	2:6 מִשְׁלֵי
	will give		for	Proverbs 2:6
				Normal English

> **Ancient חָכְמָה** H6
>
> Why is having the wisdom of Adonai important? One answer can be seen by looking at the ancient pictographs of the letters that make up the root of wisdom: ח.כ.ם.
> In ancient times, Hebrew letters were represented by pictures with special meanings.
> *Teaching below by Diana Poon (Poony).*
> (For more study, search online for Ancient Hebrew, Picto or Paleo Hebrew.)

ם	כ	ח	Modern Letter
			Ancient Letter
water	open palm	tent wall	Letter Meaning
chaos	protect/cover	fence/wall	Deeper Meaning

H7

Wisdom is a fence (ח) that protects (כ) us from chaos (ם). H8

I – Technology - Serve-A-Verse

In many of the lessons, a new piece of technology is introduced to help you learn Hebrew.

Even after learning the pronunciation tips found in this lesson, it is ALWAYS helpful to hear the Scripture being read by a native Israeli speaker. The **Serve-A-Verse** program allows you to look up a specific chapter and verse of Scripture and hear the proper Hebrew pronunciation.

The program is free, but you can purchase the paid version, **BibleInHebrew,** for one month (less than $10) with more options (including slowing down the speaker, adding vowel points, accents and other language translations). The steps to use the free software are below:

1. On your computer or smart phone, open http://www.levsoftware.com/SAV/ (Note - the web address is case sensitive!)
2. To sign up, click **Register**.
3. Fill in your information, then click **Register**.
4. They will send you an email. Open the email, and click on the link to activate your account.

5. Click **Login,** and enter your email and password.

6. Select the **Book**, **Chapter**, and **From Verse** and **To Verse.** Then click **Serve-A-Verse.**

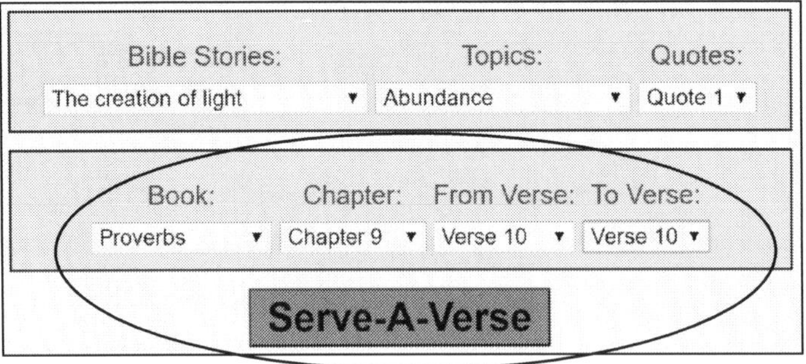

7. Click **Play** to hear the verse.

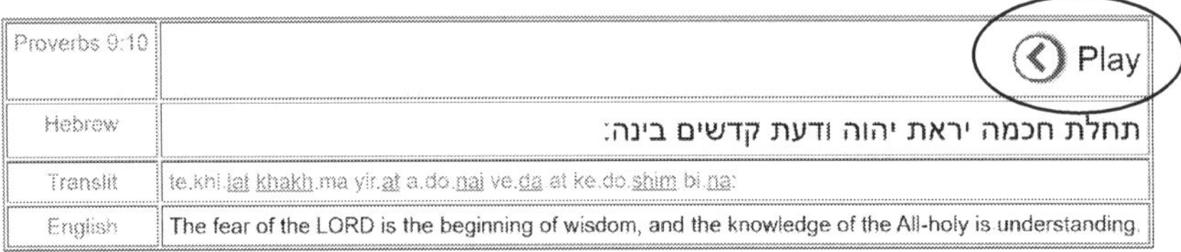

8. Try to read the Hebrew as you listen. Notice the Hebrew transliteration included.

Tic Tac Toe

GROUPS - Before starting the game, make ten game pieces – five of one color and five of another. Each player picks a color. To play the game, one player puts a piece down on a square and must read and translate the word/s. Then the opponent plays. The object is to be the first to have three pieces of their color in a row (vertical, horizontal or diagonal).

SELF-STUDY – Cut out these blocks or download the handout from https://hebrewwithjoy.com/bhj-handouts/
Use the blocks as flashcards to practice the phrases taught in the lesson.

בָּרוּךְ אַתָּה	בְּשֵׁם	מֶלֶךְ יִשְׂרָאֵל
חָכְמָה	בָּרוּךְ אַתָּה יְיָ	לֶחֶם
תּוֹדָה רַבָּה יְהוָה	בָּרוּךְ הַשֵּׁם	אֱלֹהִים

____________שֵׁם Lesson 2 Homework

In **Sephardic** Hebrew, which syllable usually receives the accent? .1
Circle the correct answer:

First *Middle* *Second-to-Last* *Last*

Complete the missing words below, then recite this beloved prayer, the "HaMotsee," in Hebrew .2
just as Jews do every Friday at sunset as they bless Adonai for their bread:

הָעוֹלָם		אֱלֹהֵינוּ		אַתָּה	בָּרוּךְ	Hebrew
the universe	king	our God	LORD	You		English

אָמֵן	הָאָרֶץ	מִן		הַמּוֹצִיא	Hebrew
	the earth	from	bread	the one who brings forth	English

Note: This and all other Hebrew blessings in this book can be heard here:
hebrewwithjoy.com/hwj-book-2-audio-files/ Click the Blessings link at the very bottom.

Circle the correct pronunciation of the following Hebrew words, then write the meaning: .3

____________ **SEEM**-kha or seem-KHA שִׂמְחָה
____________ kol or kal כָּל
____________ e-REV or **E**-rev עֶרֶב
____________ khokh-MA or khakh-MA חָכְמָה

Circle the part of a word where the Shva vowel is… .4
end middle beginning always silent? .a
end middle beginning always sounded? .b
end middle beginning usually silent? .c

For the following Hebrew words, draw syllable lines, .5
then write the English translation below:

מִתּוֹרָתֶךָ וְיִשְׁמְרֶךָ אֱלֹהִים יְבָרֶכְךָ יִשְׂרָאֵל

________ ________ ________ ________ ________
________ ________ ________

What is the meaning of the root ח.כ.ם ? .6

____

Write (in Hebrew) one word that comes from this root, then write the English meaning: .7

______________ ______________

How do the cantillation marks help you pronounce Hebrew? .8

____

Draw syllable lines in Proverbs 9:10, then read the Scripture several times. (If you are in a class, be ready to recite the scripture out loud.) Also, write the normal English meaning: .9

תְּחִלַּ֣ת חָ֭כְמָה יִרְאַ֣ת יְהוָ֑ה וְדַ֖עַת קְדֹשִׁ֣ים בִּינָֽה׃

____

What is one of your favorite English Scripture (that you DON'T already know in Hebrew)? .10
Look up the Scripture in Hebrew and practice pronouncing it.

English Scripture reference: ______________________________

Extra Technology Challenge

Create a **Serve-A-Verse** account online. (Refer to the steps in the lesson.) .11
(Or pay for one month to use **BibleInHebrew.com.**) Using either program, look up your favorite Scripture and listen to it several times. List all of the types of information that are included in the Serve-A-Verse/BibleInHebrew window:

____

____

Lesson 3 – Prefixes, Part 1

Hebrew Phrase
To your health! ("Get well!" or after a sneeze)
לַבְּרִיאוּת!

A - Vocabulary

Memorize the following words:

English	Gender	Transliteration	Hebrew	
day	ms	yom	יוֹם	A1
specific direct object marker *(no English translation – see F1)*	-	et	אֵת, אֶת	A2
heaven/s	mpl	sha-**MAI**-yeem	שָׁמַיִם	A3
earth/land	ms	**E**-retz	אֶרֶץ	A4
create/creator	ms	bo-RE	בּוֹרֵא	A5

B - Prefix ..הַ "the"

NOTE: Although many Hebrew letters can be added as prefixes to Hebrew words, for purposes of this introduction class, we will study only the most common ones: הַ, ו ,בּ, ל, מ B1

The prefix ..הַ adds "the" before a Hebrew word: B2

the name = הַשֵּׁם the = הַ

Notice that a "da-GESH" (middle dot) is added in the letter following the הַ unless it is one of these letters: (א ה ח ע ר). B3

Read the following words two times, then write the English meaning below each word: B4

הָאָרֶץ	הַשָּׁמַיִם	הַכֹּל	הַיּוֹם
________	________	________	today
________	________	________	(the day)

Notice that when a prefix is added to a Hebrew word, the vowels in the word <u>may</u> change. For example, אֶרֶץ means "earth/land" and הָאָרֶץ means "the earth/land." B5

C – Prefix ..ו "and"

The prefix ..ו (וְ וַ וָ וִ) adds "and" before most Hebrew words. C1

Note that ..ו changes to ..וּ (soft "oo" sound) if it comes before these letters: ב, מ, פ
or if the next letter has a Shva under it.

Read the following phrases two times, then write the English meaning below each phrase:

שָׁלוֹם וְאַהֲבָה   אַהֲבָה וּבְרָכוֹת   חָכְמָה וְשִׂמְחָה C2

______________   ______________   ______________

______________   ______________   ______________

The Vav, the Tabernacle and the Torah C3

The word "Vav" was used in Exodus 27:9-10 to refer to the hooks of silver that were used to hold the curtain that enclosed the Tabernacle. Just as the Tabernacle was the dwelling place of Adonai, the Torah is the dwelling place of His Word today. To honor these "Vavs" (silver hooks), Torah scribes start each column with a Vav, thus "hooking" the columns together. Each Torah parchment page is made from the skin of a Kosher animal and cannot contain any errors. In fact, if an error is made, the page must be buried in a גְּנִיזָה (g-nee-ZA); a text cemetery!

D – Prefix ..בְּ ..בַּ "in/with"

The prefix ..בְּ adds "in" or "with" before a Hebrew word. D1
Usually you need to add "a" or "an" to translate correctly into English because there are no Hebrew words for "a" or "an"!
For example: בְּאֶרֶץ = "in (a) land"

..בַּ combines the prefixes הַ + בְּ D2
..בַּ always adds "in the" or "with the" before a Hebrew word.
For example: בָּאָרֶץ = "in the land" instead of "in a land"

בְּשֵׁם = is an exception as it translates into "in (the) name." D3

Read the following words two times, then write the English meaning below each one: D4

בְּשֵׁם   בְּשִׂמְחָה   בְּאֶרֶץ   בָּאָרֶץ   בְּרֵאשִׁית

______________   ______________   ______________   ______________   ______________

______________   ______________   ______________   ______________   beginning

E – Root ב.ר.א

Write the missing English word below:

Words from the Root		
(ms)	בּוֹרֵא	E2
created (ms) past	בָּרָא	E3
health	בְּרִיאוּת	E4
to (your) health! In Israel- "Get well" or after someone sneezes	לַבְּרִיאוּת !	E5

Root Meaning	Root	
create, shape, form	ב.ר.א 54X	E1

The "**Kiddush**" קִדּוּשׁ (Sanctification) בְּרָכָה (Blessing) is recited by Jews around the world every עֶרֶב שַׁבָּת (Sabbath [Friday] evening) at sunset as they lift their wine glasses and thank Adonai before their Shabbat meal. E6

Write the missing Hebrew and English words below, then circle the word from the root ב.ר.א: E7

הָעוֹלָם		אֱלֹהֵינוּ	יְהוָה	אַתָּה		Hebrew
(of) ______ universe	king	our God		You	blessed	English

אָמֵן	הַגָּפֶן	פְּרִי	בּוֹרֵא	Hebrew
	(of) _____ vine	fruit		English

F – Specific Direct Object Marker את

The amazing את is found over 7000 times in Scripture! You may see it as אֵת or אֶת and while it does not translate into English, it does have a unique job in Hebrew. It tells you that the Hebrew word which follows it is a **specific** direct object (the direct object is the word that receives the action of the sentence). F1

For example, Genesis 1:1 says, "God created **the** heavens and **the** earth." What did God create? Not just "a" heaven or "an" earth (not specific), but "the" heavens and "the" earth. (specific!) People and places are also specific. F2

Translate into proper English (notice the verb comes before the subject!): F3

בָּרָא אֱלֹהִים אֶת אַבְרָהָם

_________________ Abraham

בָּרָא יְהוָה אֶת יִשְׂרָאֵל

____

G – Reading Scripture

You can now read and translate the first Scripture in the Bible!
Fill in the missing English translations, then write the Scripture in normal English:

הָאָרֶץ׃	וְאֵת	הַשָּׁמַיִם	אֵת	אֱלֹהִים	בָּרָא	בְּרֵאשִׁית	בְּרֵאשִׁית 1:1	G1
			----			In (the) beginning	Genesis 1:1	G2
							Normal English	G3

G4

Word Order

Biblical Hebrew vs. Modern Hebrew

In English, the subject of the sentence comes before the verb (as in "GOD created…"). But, in Biblical Hebrew, as you can see in Genesis 1:1, the verb comes before the subject (as in "created GOD…"). What about Modern Hebrew? Surprisingly, the subject comes before the verb in Modern Hebrew, just like in English!

Read these Scriptures from Genesis 1:1-3 out loud, then circle the prefixes in line 1: G5

1 בְּרֵאשִׁית בָּרָא אֱלֹהִים אֵת הַשָּׁמַיִם וְאֵת הָאָרֶץ׃

2 וְהָאָרֶץ הָיְתָה תֹהוּ וָבֹהוּ וְחֹשֶׁךְ עַל־פְּנֵי תְהוֹם
וְרוּחַ אֱלֹהִים מְרַחֶפֶת עַל־פְּנֵי הַמָּיִם׃

3 וַיֹּאמֶר אֱלֹהִים יְהִי אוֹר וַיְהִי־אוֹר׃

Genesis 1:1-3 In the beginning God created the heavens and the earth. Now the earth was chaos and waste, darkness was on the surface of the deep, and the *Ruach Elohim* was hovering upon the surface of the water. Then God said, "Let there be light!" and there was light. (TLV) G6

H – Technology - Bible Hub

Bible Hub is another free program that can be used on your computer or cell phone. Here is an example of what you can see in Bible Hub: H1

H2

Bible Hub steps:

1. On your computer or cell phone, open **www.biblehub.com.** H3
2. Click on **Interlinear** to see the English right under the Hebrew.

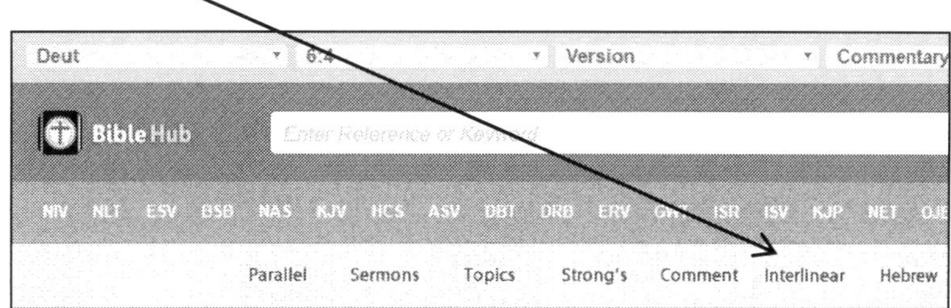

3. In the white Search box, type in the Scripture reference, then click the Search button.

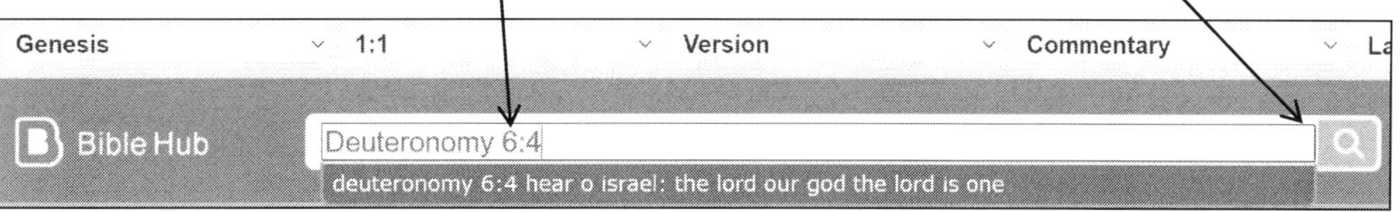

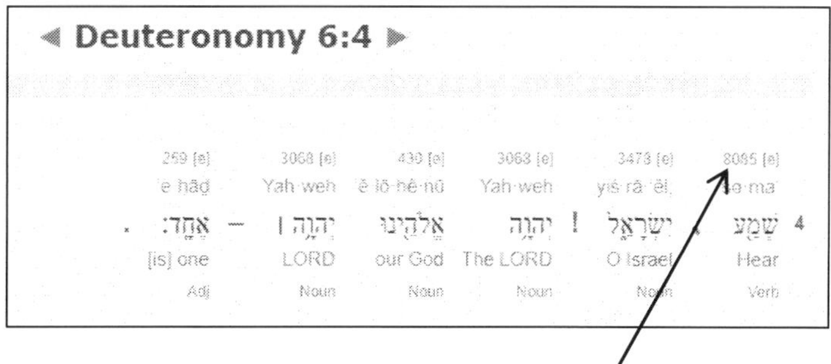

4. To see the Strong's definitions, click on the Strong's number above the word to see the root and the many translations of the Hebrew word used throughout Scripture.
5. To return back to the Scripture, click the back button. ←

Flashcard Practice

Many people find success memorizing new information by using flashcards, so the flashcards will be the learning activity for Lesson 3. You have two options:

1. Cut out the flashcards for Lessons 1-3 in Appendix F page 127.
2. Download a complete copy of the flashcards from the *Hebrew with Joy!* website: https://hebrewwithjoy.com/bhj-handouts/
   *If you download and print, try to use cardstock and print double-sided.

Practice using the flashcards by yourself or ask a classmate, family member or friend to test you. Notice that the Lesson # is included on each card.

NOTE: If you are an audio learner, use the audio files to memorize new words. The files can also be downloaded to your computer or phone from the *Hebrew with Joy!* website: https://hebrewwithjoy.com/bhj-audios/

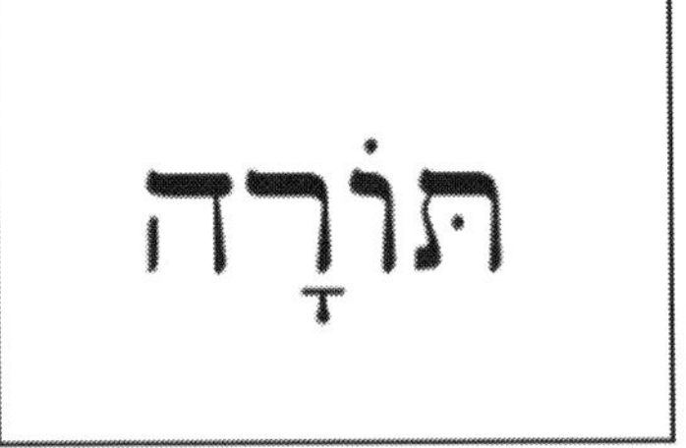

instruction
fs 1

Lesson 3 Homework

Translate the following phrases into English:

	הָאָרֶץ	.1
	לַבְּרִיאוּת!	.2
	בְּשֵׁם	.3
	הַשָּׁמַיִם	.4
	בָּרָא אֱלֹהִים	.5
	הַשֵּׁם	.6
	בְּאֶרֶץ	.7
	בָּאָרֶץ	.8
	חָכְמָה וְשִׂמְחָה	.9

What is the purpose of the אֵת or אֶת? .10

____

Read the following Scriptures from Genesis 1:4-6 out loud several times.
Then underline the roots and words you know and (CIRCLE) the prefixes you know: .11

4 וַיַּרְא אֱלֹהִים אֶת־הָאוֹר כִּי־טוֹב וַיַּבְדֵּל
אֱלֹהִים בֵּין הָאוֹר וּבֵין הַחֹשֶׁךְ׃

5 וַיִּקְרָא אֱלֹהִים ׀ לָאוֹר יוֹם וְלַחֹשֶׁךְ קָרָא
לָיְלָה וַיְהִי־עֶרֶב וַיְהִי־בֹקֶר יוֹם אֶחָד׃

6 וַיֹּאמֶר אֱלֹהִים יְהִי רָקִיעַ בְּתוֹךְ
הַמָּיִם וִיהִי מַבְדִּיל בֵּין מַיִם לָמָיִם׃

What is the meaning of the root ב.ר.א ? .13

____

Write (in Hebrew) one word that comes from this root, then write the English meaning: .14

________________ ________________

Look up the verse you chose in Lesson 2 homework (that you don't already know in Hebrew). Your challenge is to memorize this verse in Hebrew before the end of class! .15

English book and verse: ______________________

Write your Scripture in English: .16

____
____
____

In **Bible Hub** or another reference, look up your Scripture. .17
Draw syllable lines to help you pronounce each word as you complete the chart:

					Hebrew
					English

					Hebrew
					English

					Hebrew
					English

If you are using **Bible Hub**, choose one word from the Scripture and click on the Strong's number above it. Then, complete the chart below: .18

Several Meanings of the Root	Root Letters	Strongs #	English Word	Hebrew Word

Lesson 4 – Prefixes, Part 2

עַם יִשְׂרָאֵל חַי!
The people of Israel live!

A - Vocabulary

Memorize the following words:

English	*Gender*	Transliteration	Hebrew	
I*	*ms, fs*	*a-NEE*	אֲנִי	A1
you	*ms* *fs*	*a-TA* *at*	אַתָּה אַתְּ	A2
he, it	*ms*	*hoo*	הוּא	A3
guard/keep	*ms*	*sho-MER*	שׁוֹמֵר	A4
my beloved	*ms*	*do-DEE*	דוֹדִי	A5

*In Biblical Hebrew, אָנֹכִי is another form of "I".
Complete list of pronouns is on Appendix J, p. 140.

B – Prefix ..לְ "to/for"

The prefix ..לְ adds "to" or "for" before a Hebrew word: B1
to life = לְחַיִּים

Read the following phrases two times, then write the English meaning below each phrase:

לְיִשְׂרָאֵל לְדוֹדִי לְשִׂמְחָה לַבְּרִיאוּת B2

__________ __________ __________ __________

__________ __________ __________ __________

B3

לְחַיִּים

לְחַיִּים in Hebrew is a toast meaning "to life." When a Jewish couple becomes engaged, the celebration itself is called a לְחַיִּים. During the wedding, the bride circles the groom seven times as seven blessings are read. This is believed to tear down any walls of separation between them and give her entrance into the depths of her beloved's heart. At the end of the ceremony, לְחַיִּים is proclaimed by one and all as the groom breaks the wine glass.

Fill in the English words from this wedding Scripture, Song of Songs 6:3: B4

לִי	וְדוֹדִי	לְדוֹדִי	אֲנִי	Hebrew
______ me	______ ______ ______	______ ______ ______		English
				Normal English

The "Ketubah" כְּתֻבָּה is the marriage contract in a Jewish wedding. Many Jewish couples frame their beautiful כְּתֻבָּה and display it in their homes as a reminder of the vows made to one another. (See the example below. Can you read the Hebrew?) B5

B6

אֲנִי לְדוֹדִי וְדוֹדִי לִי

This Ketubah witnesses before Adonai that on
the ______________, ______________,
the groom, ______________, and the bride, ______________,
said to each other, "You're my lover and my best friend. Today we are united in
the Holy Covenant of Marriage as servants of Adonai,
by the Torah, the laws of Moses. I promise to always love you,
to respect you and to be faithful to you as long as we live."

As it is written in the Torah of the Lord: "Therefore let a man leave his father and
mother and cleave to his wife, and they shall become one flesh." Gen 2:24
Adonai's Word will be our light as we journey through life together.
We will love Adonai with all our hearts, minds, and souls.
We will honor the Torah and Adonai.

Bride Groom

Official

Witness Witness

Elul אֱלוּל

B7

Ever wonder why there are a lot of weddings in the month of "Elul," the Hebrew month preceding the Fall Feasts? One theory is that אֱלוּל can be interpreted as an acronym for אֲנִי לְדוֹדִי וְדוֹדִי לִי - "I am my beloved's and my beloved is mine" (Song of Songs 6:3). A beautiful tradition is that many Jewish wedding rings are inscribed with this beloved verse. Thus, Elul is the month of love and relationships; the perfect time to renew our covenant relationship with our precious ADONAI.

C – Prefix ..מ "from"

The prefix ..מ adds "from" before many Hebrew words. C1
Note that there are many Hebrew words that start with a Mem
where the Mem is not a prefix. For example: מֶלֶךְ

Read the following phrases two times, then write the English meaning below each phrase: C2

מִתּוֹרָתֶךָ	מִתּוֹרָה	מִכָּל	מֵיְהוָה
_______ your	______________	______________	______________
______________	______________	______________	______________

***In these last two lessons, we have studied the most common prefixes. C3
A complete list is included in Appendix H, page 138, at the end of the book.

D – Root שׁ.מ.ר

Words from the Root		
(ms)	שׁוֹמֵר	D2
guard/keep (fs)	שׁוֹמֶרֶת	D3
guards/watchmen (mpl)	שׁוֹמְרִים	D4
guards/watchmen (fpl)	שׁוֹמְרוֹת	D5

Root Meaning	Root	
guard, keep	שׁ.מ.ר 468X	D1

Fill in the missing words from this Scripture: D6

רָע	מִכָּל־	יִשְׁמָרְךָ		תְּהִלִּים 121:7
evil/harm		will ________ you	LORD	Psalm 121:7
				Normal English

E – Simple Sentences

In both Biblical and Modern Hebrew, there are no Hebrew words for "is," "am," "are," "a" or "an." As a result, sentences can be as short as two words! E1
For example: "You **are a** guard." אַתָּה שׁוֹמֵר.

Remember that the word order may be different than normal English! E2
For example: "He **is** blessed." בָּרוּךְ הוּא.

Translate the following Hebrew sentences into normal English:

	הוּא שׁוֹמֵר מִיִּשְׂרָאֵל.	E3
	בָּרוּךְ אַתָּה.	E4
	אֲנִי שׁוֹמֵר בְּיִשְׂרָאֵל.	E5

Translate the following Hebrew words in the most beloved Hebrew Scripture, then write the normal English: E6

אֶחָד	יְהוָה	אֱלֹהֵינוּ	יְהוָה	יִשְׂרָאֵל	שְׁמַע	דְּבָרִים 6:4
one		our ________				Deuteronomy 6:4
						Normal English

Circle the extra English words needed in the normal English above (that don't translate to Hebrew): E7

E8

שְׁמַע

Deuteronomy 6:4 *"Hear, Israel, the Lord our God, the Lord is One."* To Jews, the "שְׁמַע" is the most important prayer in Judaism. It reminds them of the key principle of the faith: there is only one God. Traditionally, while praying the שְׁמַע, Jews outside of Israel stand and face the Land of Israel; in Israel, they face Jerusalem; and in Jerusalem, they face the original Temple Mount. The שְׁמַע is also found in the Mezuzah (prayer box on doorposts) and in the phylacteries (leather boxes worn on the arm and forehead).

F – Reading Scriptures

Read these Scriptures from Deuteronomy 6:4-5 out loud: F1

4 שְׁמַע יִשְׂרָאֵל יְהוָה אֱלֹהֵינוּ יְהוָה ׀ אֶחָד׃

5 וְאָהַבְתָּ אֵת יְהוָה אֱלֹהֶיךָ בְּכָל־לְבָבְךָ
וּבְכָל־נַפְשְׁךָ וּבְכָל־מְאֹדֶךָ׃

Deuteronomy 6:4-5 F2

Hear O Israel, the LORD our God, the LORD is one.
And you shall love *ADONAI* your God with all your heart and with all your soul and with all your strength.

G – Technology – Translation Programs

One of the goals of this class is encouraging you to use GOD's holy language G1
to write or speak your own personal prayers to Adonai. An excellent tool
to help you is an English-Hebrew translation program or app.

Here are my favorites (both of which have a free version).

1. **Google Translate** can be used as an app on your cell phone or a web page on G2
your computer at https://translate.google.com/. After typing the English, you
will see the Hebrew translation (without vowels).

2. **iTranslate** is a cell phone app only available on iPhones. Vowels are not
included, but the translation does have an audio button to hear the Hebrew
translation spoken by a native Israeli.

The basic steps to use both of these: G3

Make sure that English and Hebrew are selected as the two languages. .1
Click in the English box and type your sentence or phrase. .2
Click the Translate button. .3
View the Hebrew translation (without vowels). .4
If you are using **iTranslate**, click on the audio button to hear the Hebrew. .5

G4

Where did all the vowels go?

Biblical Hebrew vs. Modern Hebrew

Why don't the translation programs include vowels? In Israel today, young children learning to read Modern Hebrew are introduced to the letters and the vowels. However, once they know the Alef-Bet (alphabet) and have a good vocabulary, the vowels are dropped! The children can still read because they understand the context of the sentences. So, in Modern Hebrew, there are no vowels; no vowels in books or newspapers or online! Does this seem impossible? Try translating this into English:

שמע ישראל ______________________

Thankfully, most Hebrew Bibles do include vowels!

Memory Game

Either cut this page into pieces or download the game from https://hebrewwithjoy.com/bhj-handouts/, then print on cardstock (if possible) and cut out the pieces. Place the pieces on a table with the words facing down and mix well. Player 1 turns over two cards to see if they match (Hebrew prefix with English meaning). If they do, player 1 keeps the pair and turns over two more. If they don't match, player 2 takes a turn. Play continues until all pairs are matched. Player with the most pairs wins. You can even play this game if you are studying by yourself.

וְ..	in the/ with the	לְ..
..the	to/for	הַ..
and	מִ..	in/with
בְּ..	from	בַּ..

Lesson 4 Homework שֵׁם__________

1. Write the English translation for the following Hebrew prefixes:

הַ..   בְּ..   בַּ..   לְ..   וְ..   מִ..

_______ _______ _______ _______ _______ _______

Translate the following phrases into English (remember to use correct English word order):

.2	בָּרוּךְ הָאָרֶץ.	
.3	אַתָּה שׁוֹמֵר.	
.4	בָּרוּךְ אַתָּה יְהוָה.	
.5	אַתְּ מִיִשְׂרָאֵל.	
.6	בָּרָא אֱלֹהִים אֵת הַשָּׁמַיִם.	
.7	אַתָּה הַמֶּלֶךְ.	
.8	הוּא בְּאֶרֶץ.	
.9	הוּא בַּאֶרֶץ.	
.10	בָּרוּךְ הוּא.	

11. Which English words do not translate into Hebrew?

____

12. What is the meaning of the root ש.מ.ר ? ____________

13. Write (in Hebrew) two words that comes from this root, then write the English meanings:

______________ ______________

______________ ______________

Read the following Psalm out loud twice. Then, complete the English meanings. .14
Finally, write the Scripture in normal English.

הָאָרֶץ	כָּל-	לַיהוָה	שִׁירוּ	חָדָשׁ	שִׁיר	לַיהוָה	שִׁירוּ	תְּהִלִּים 96:1
			sing	new	song		sing	Psalm 96:1
								normal English

In the Scripture above, **circle** the prefixes, and <u>underline</u> the words and roots you know: .15

Using one of the Hebrew translation programs in Section G, write an English prayer and .16
translate to Hebrew telling Adonai what you are thankful for. Write the Hebrew translation below (<u>you don't need to write the vowels</u>.) Ideas… I am thankful for life, friends & family members, health, congregation etc.):

____

____

____

____

What is the English translation of your prayer? .17

____

____

____

Which Hebrew translation program did you use? .18

____

Lesson 5 – Plural Suffixes

Hebrew Greetings	
Welcome!/Blessed is the comer **ms** (new baby boy)	בָּרוּךְ הַבָּא!
Welcome!/Blessed are the comers **mpl** (newly married)	בְּרוּכִים הַבָּאִים!

A - Vocabulary

Memorize the following words:

English	*Gender*	Transliteration	Hebrew	
son/child	*ms*	*ben*	בֵּן	A1
commandment	*fs*	*meets-VA*	מִצְוָה	A2
appointed time/season	*ms*	*mo-ED*	מוֹעֵד	A3
word/thing	*ms*	*da-VAR*	דָּבָר	A4
week	*ms*	*sha-**VOO**-a*	שָׁבוּעַ	A5
we	*plural***	*a-**NAKH**-noo, **A**-noo*	אֲנַחְנוּ, אָנוּ	A6

*The complete list of pronouns is in Appendix J, page 140.
** The Hebrew pronouns for "we" are not gender specific. Either word could apply to groups of males, females or mixed groups

B - Gender

In Hebrew, nouns and verbs are either: B1
masculine (זָכָר za-KHAR) or feminine (נְקֵבָה n-ke-VA).

As a general rule, words ending in ה or ת are feminine. B2
In most cases, words that **don't** end in ה or ת are masculine.
*As you might guess, there will be exceptions to these gender rules.

For each of the following words, circle M for masculine or F for feminine, B3
then write the English meaning below each word:

שָׁבוּעַ	מִצְוָה	מוֹעֵד	שַׁבָּת	בְּרָכָה	B4
M or F	M or F	M or F	M or F	M or F	
________	________	________	________	________	

אֱמוּנָה	שָׁנָה	דָּבָר	יוֹם	שׁוֹמֵר	B5
M or F	M or F	M or F	M or F	M or F	
faith	year	________	________	________	

Faith, Truth and Amen! B6

The righteous will live by his faith. Habakkuk 2:4

The root of the Hebrew word for "faith," אֱמוּנָה is א.מ.ן. What is amazing is that this is also the root for "truth," אֱמֶת and for "Amen" ("so be it") אָמֵן. So, when we say "Amen" in agreement with a prayer or a statement, we are actually saying that we truthfully believe what is being said, and we have faith that it will actually come to be.

C – Masculine Plural Suffix ◌ִים

The ◌ִים suffix (ending) indicates that a word is masculine plural. C1
This suffix can also apply to mixed groups (both males and females).

Vowels and letters may change in the plural form. For example, יוֹם (day) changes C2
to יָמִים (days) and בֵּן (son/child) changes to בָּנִים (sons/children).

Read the following masculine words, then write the English meaning below each word: C3

יָמִים	שׁוֹמְרִים	דְּבָרִים	מוֹעֲדִים	בָּנִים
________	________	________	________	________
		________	________	

Majestic Plurals C4

*"The **heavens** declare the glory of **God**, and the sky shows His handiwork."* Psalm 19:1(2)

As you have learned, the Hebrew word for "heaven" is שָׁמַיִם and the Hebrew word for "GOD" is אֱלֹהִים. Both words are singular, but the meanings of these words, which refer to both quality and quantity, are **SO BIG** that even in the singular they have a plural ending! We do indeed serve an infinite, awesome, mighty GOD! Hallelujah!

D – Feminine Plural Suffix וֹת..

The וֹת.. suffix shows that a word is feminine plural. D1

If the singular Hebrew word ends in ה, the ה drops when the וֹת.. is added. D2
For example, בְּרָכָה (blessing) changes to בְּרָכוֹת (blessings).

Read the following feminine words, then write the English meaning below each word: D3

מִצְוֹת*	שַׁבָּתוֹת	בְּרָכוֹת
________	________	________

*EXCEPTION -The correct pronunciation for מִצְוֹת is "meets-VOT." In this word, the Vav makes two different sounds: both the "v" sound and the "o" sound.

E – Plural Suffix Exceptions

Occasionally, a feminine word will have a masculine plural ending **or** a masculine word will have a feminine plural ending. E1

Circle the gender for each word, then write the plural meaning (for help, see B4-B5):

English Plural Meaning	Plural	Gender	Singular	
	שָׁנִים	M or F	שָׁנָה	E2
	שֵׁמוֹת	M or F	שֵׁם	E3
	שָׁבוּעוֹת	M or F	שָׁבוּעַ	E4

Why did Adonai create the sun, moon and stars? Fill in the blanks to answer:

וְשָׁנִים	וּלְיָמִים	וּלְמוֹעֲדִים	לְאֹתֹת	וְהָיוּ	בְּרֵאשִׁית 1:14b	E5
			_____ signs	_____ (they) will be	Genesis 1:14b	
					Normal English	E6

F – Root - ד.ב.ר

Read each word twice, then fill in the missing word:

speak, word, thing	ד.ב.ר 1439X	F1
	דָּבָר	F2
speak/talk - ms	מְדַבֵּר	F3
in the desert (book of Numbers)	בַּמִּדְבָּר	F4
words (book of Deuteronomy)	דְּבָרִים	F5
10 Words (10 Commandments)	עֲשֶׂרֶת הַדְּבָרִים	F6

F7

In the Wilderness

Although the desert seems (on the surface) to be a place that is hostile to life, the Hebrew language shows us that the spiritual wilderness experience can be a very valuable time of growing in our relationship with the Lord. The word "meed-BAR" (desert), מִדְבָּר contains the exact same letters as "m-da-BER" מְדַבֵּר which is the Hebrew word for "speak or talk." It is in the wilderness times of our lives that God can speak a "Word in due season" to our hearts. *(Thanks to Hannah Nesher,* Voice for Israel, www.voiceforisrael.net)

G – The Tanakh

Tanakh תָּנָ"ךְ

In your study of Hebraic roots, you may have discovered the **Tanakh** (also called the Hebrew Bible or Old Testament). **Tanakh** is an **acronym** using the first letter of three different words. It is taken from the names of the three divisions of the Hebrew Bible: G1

T: to-RA ת תּוֹרָה (Instruction)

N: n-vee-EEM נ נְבִיאִים (Prophets)

K: k-too-VEEM ך כְּתוּבִים (Writings)

(Note: The 2 apostrophes in תנ"ך show it is an acronym.)

The following chart includes the first five books from the Tanakh (known as the תּוֹרָה) plus Psalms and Proverbs. The complete list is in Appendix K, page 141-142. G2

Fill in the blanks in the following chart then circle the plural Hebrew names:

Hebrew Meaning	Transliteration	Hebrew Word	English Name	
	b-re-SHEET	בְּרֵאשִׁית	Genesis	G3
	sh-MOT	שְׁמוֹת	Exodus	G4
and He called	*va-yeek-RA*	וַיִּקְרָא	Leviticus	G5
in the desert/ wilderness	*ba-meed-BAR*	בַּמִּדְבָּר		G6
	d-va-REEM	דְּבָרִים		G7
psalms	*t-hee-LEEM*	תְּהִלִּים		G8
proverbs	*meesh-LAY*	מִשְׁלֵי	Proverbs	G9

H – Technology - Blue Letter Bible

Many of you are taking this course so that you can read your favorite Scripture verses in Hebrew. Although there are many online Bibles available, I will share my favorite, the **Blue Letter Bible.** H1

It is a free computer and cell phone app (www.blueletterbible.org) that can include English and Hebrew translations side-by-side (in parallel). The Hebrew translation includes the vowel points, and individual Hebrew words can be selected to see the Strong's Interlinear root information. H2

Blue Letter Bible offers many English translations including the "Hebrew Names Version" HNV (which is used in the following steps). Feel free to use your favorite English version. H3

The Hebrew version selected is the "Westminster Leningrad Codex" (WLC), which includes the vowel points and is widely used. You can choose any of the WLC options (ie. WLC/BYZ, WLC/MG) H4

Note: the WLC will only work in the Tanakh; you will see Greek in the New Testament.

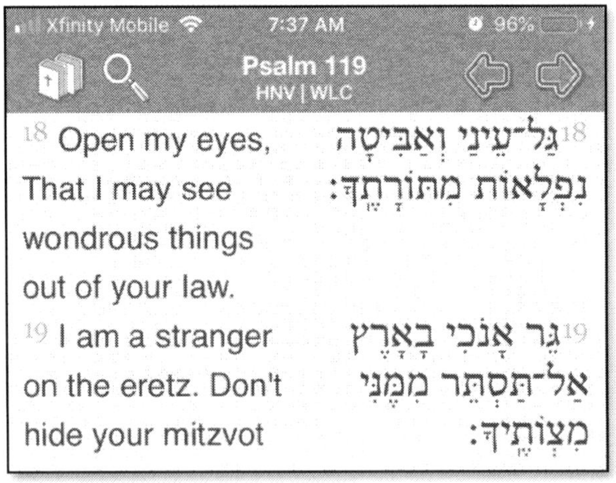

H5

Note - The steps on the next page walk you through the setup and use of the Blue Letter Bible on an **iPhone** . Android phone steps are different! They are found **after** the iPhone steps. Make sure you are following the correct steps for your phone. The setup takes a bit of time, but once it is done, the app is amazing! H6

Steps for iPhones

1. On your iPhone, download the **Blue Letter Bible,** then open the app.

2. **To set up the parallel view and select Bible versions,** click the parallel button.

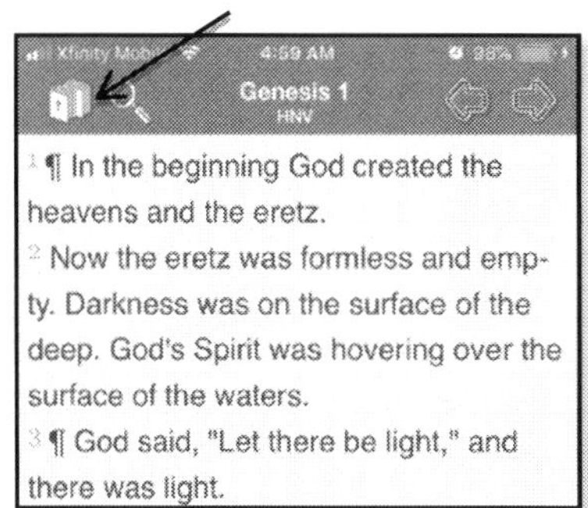

3. Click on **Manage Bibles**.

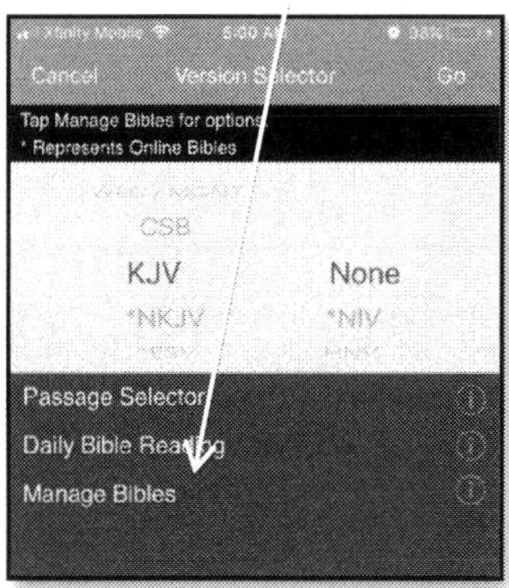

4. Scroll down & click on your favorite English translation (if your favorite isn't there, you can search for it in the next step).

5. Scroll down to locate one of the WLC Hebrew Bibles. Then click on the **down arrow** and choose **download**. If needed, also download an English Bible (e.g. HNV).

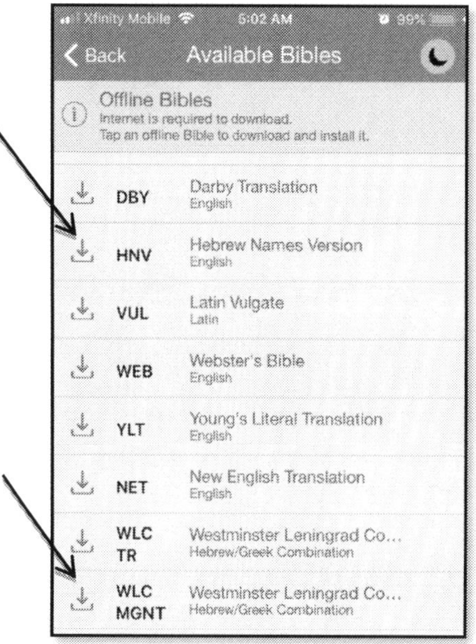

6. Always click the **Back** button to return to the last step.

7. Select your primary English Bible then click **Back.**

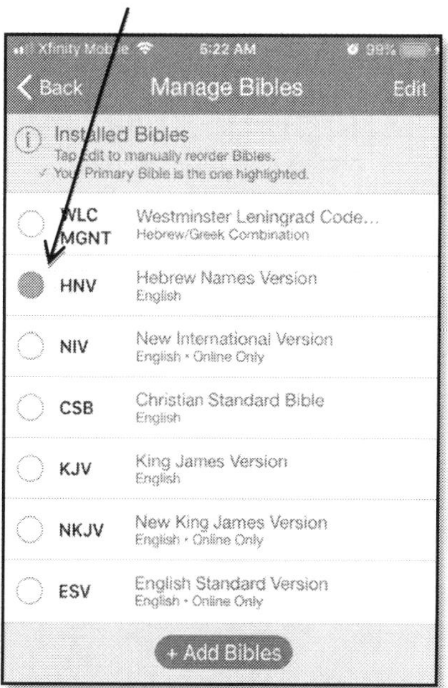

8. On the left side, select your favorite English translation; on the right side, select a WLC version.

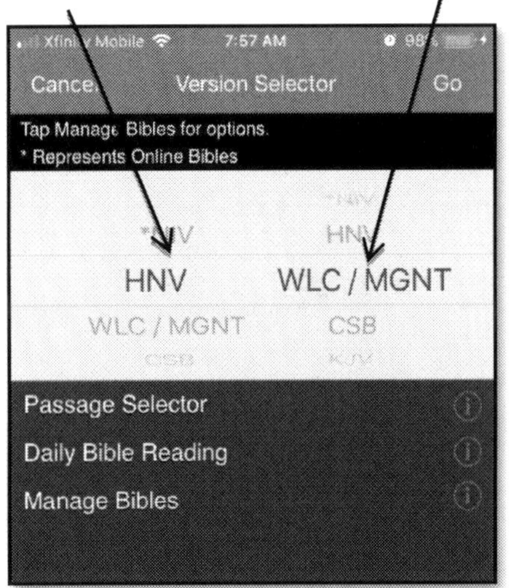

9. Click on **GO** – you are now set up!

10. **<u>To use the app</u>**, open it, then click on the Scripture reference.

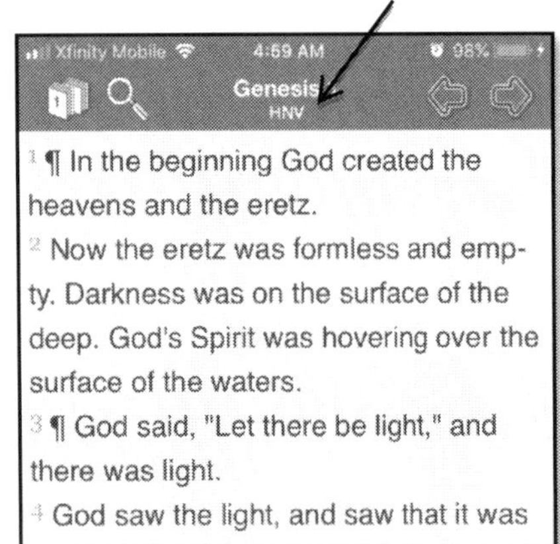

11. Select **OT** or **NT,** then select the book you want. (You will only see Hebrew in the **OT.**)

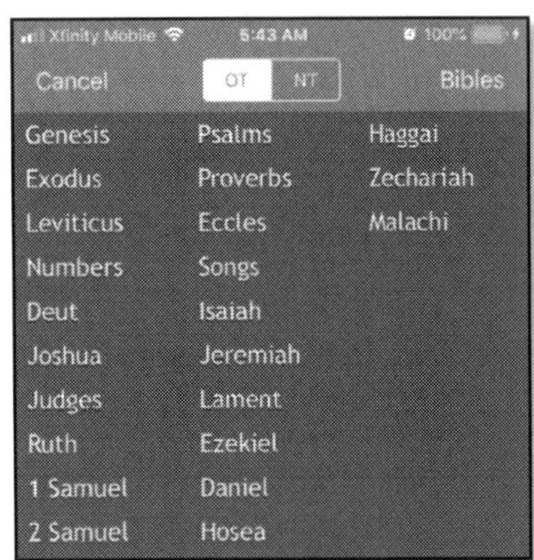

12. Select the chapter you want, then scroll down to select a verse.

13. To use the interlinear, click on the Hebrew Scripture.

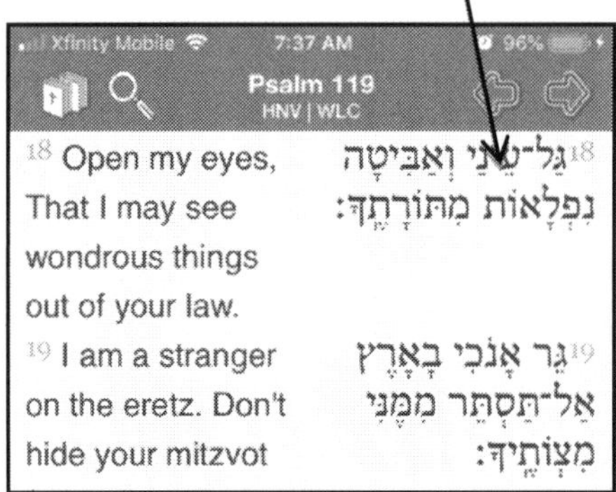

14. Click on **Interlinear/Concordance.**

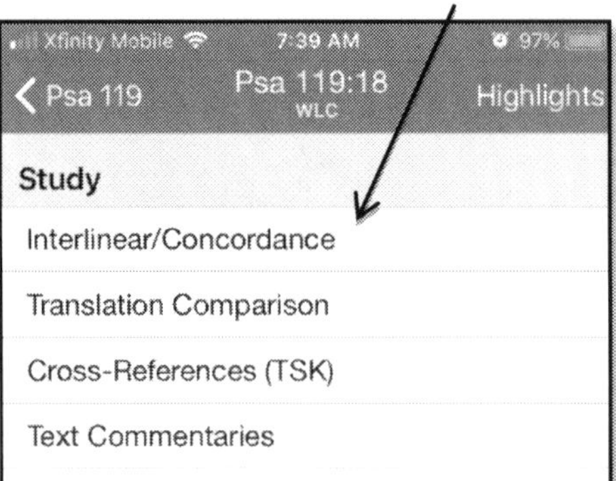

15. To see the Strong's Concordance, click on the **Strong's** number.

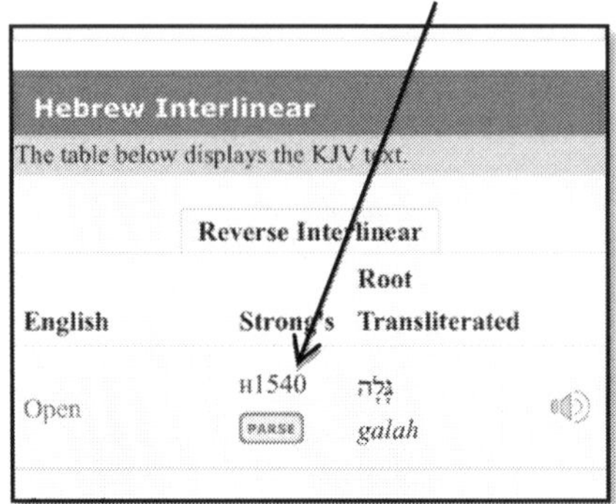

16. Always click the Back button to return to the last step.

Steps for Android Phones:

1. Download and open the **Blue Letter Bible** app.
2. Press the open Bible icon on the top left.

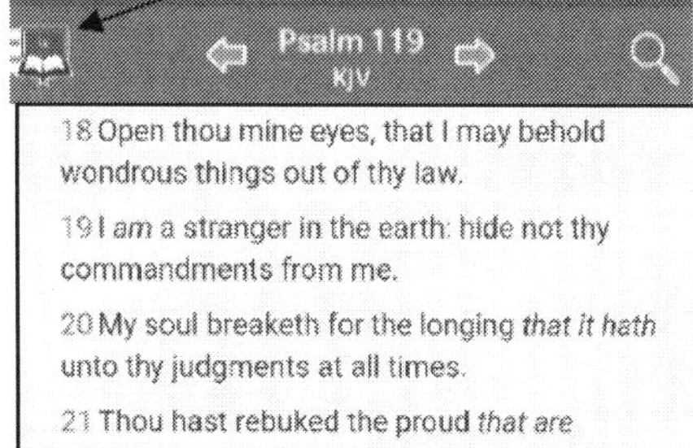

3. Choose "My Bibles."

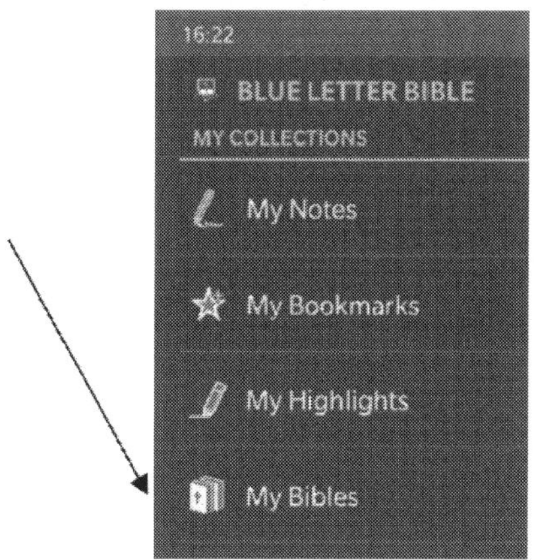

4. Scroll down to choose your "Primary" English Bible.

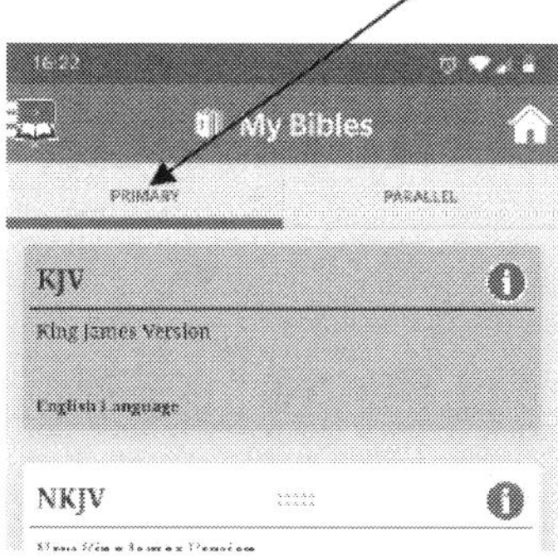

5. Click on "Parallel."

6. Scroll to choose **WLC/MGNT**.

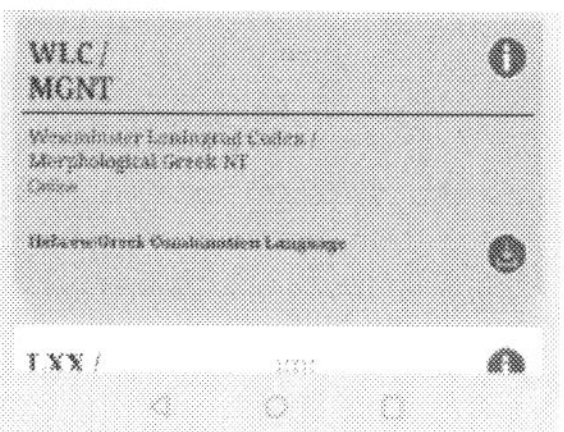

7. Then hit the "Back" button. Now you will see the verse in parallel – English and Hebrew

***IMPORTANT!
You will only see Hebrew when you are looking at an Old Testament Scripture. Greek will appear in the New Testament.

8. **To use the app**, open it, then click on the Scripture reference.

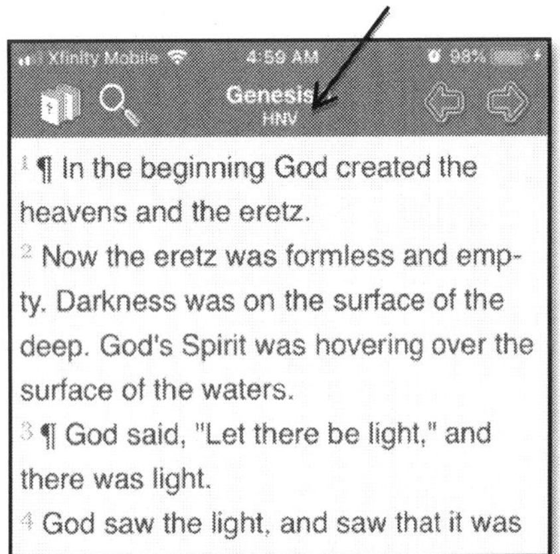

9. Select **OT** or **NT,** then select the book you want. (You will only see Hebrew in the **OT**.)

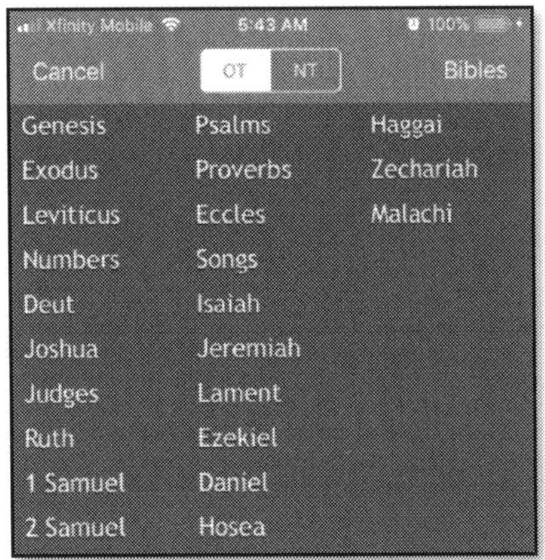

10. Select the chapter you want, then scroll down to select a verse.

11. To use the interlinear, click on the Hebrew Scripture.

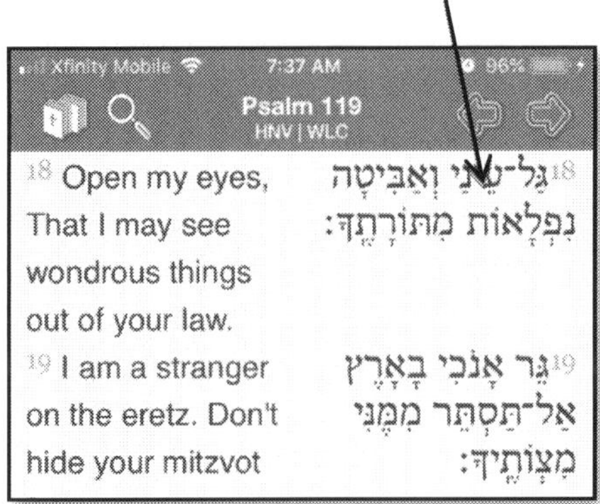

12. Click on **Interlinear.**

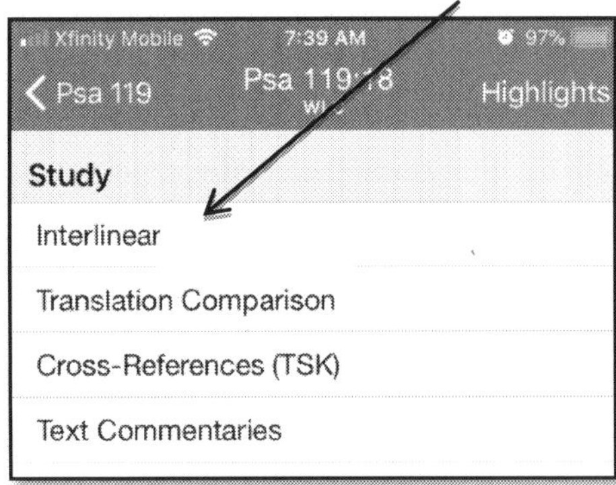

13. To see the Strong's Concordance, click on the **Strong's** number.

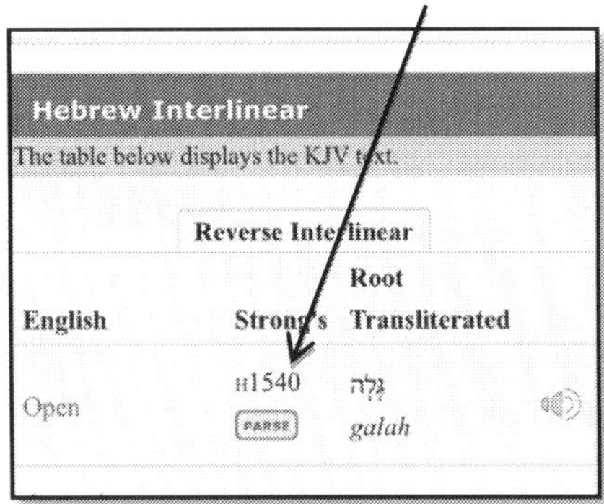

14. Always click the Back button to return to the last step.

Match the Plurals!

Team Game: Photocopy two copies of this page or download and print 2 copies from the *Hebrew with Joy!* website. Cut out the pieces. Divide the students into 2 teams, then give each team a complete set. The teams turn the pieces face down on a table. On a signal from the leader, teams turn over all of the pieces and try to match the Hebrew with the English plurals separating the pairs into masculine or feminine piles. First team to match and separate all 9 sets wins the game.

Individual Students: Copy and cut these pieces as flashcards to test yourself.

מוֹעֲדִים	days	שׁוֹמְרִים
appointed times/seasons	blessings	שָׁבוּעוֹת
מִצְוֹת	בָּנִים	יָמִים
דְּבָרִים	sons	commandments
guards/ watchmen	שֵׁמוֹת	words/things
weeks	names	בְּרָכוֹת

Lesson 5 Homework

Translate the following words into עִבְרִית to complete the crossword puzzle:

				C		1
						2
				A		3
░			B			4
░	░	D				5
░	░					6
░	░					7

appointed times	1
guards/watchmen	2
weeks	3
book of Deuteronomy	4
commandments	5
book of Exodus	6
days	7

		כ		
D	C		B	A

What is the English word from the puzzle? ____________________

____ ____ What are the 2 most common endings for a feminine <u>singular</u> word? .9

________ What is the most common Hebrew masculine <u>plural</u> suffix? .10

_______ What is the most common Hebrew feminine <u>plural</u> suffix? .11

____________________________ What is the meaning of the root ד.ב.ר ? .12

Write three Hebrew words that come from this root and their English meanings: .13

_____________ _____________ _____________

_____________ _____________ _____________

Set up the **Blue Letter Bible** on your smartphone. Make sure that you see both the English and Hebrew side-by-side. (Or use a Strong's Concordance). Now look up Exodus 31:16. Click on the Hebrew and then click on the Interlinear/Concordance. For each of the words below, click on the Hebrew word to see the Strong's root information: .14

Write three meanings of עָשָׂה: .15

____

Write three meanings of דּוֹר: .16

____

Mid Quiz

At the beginning of this course, you took a Pre-Quiz to see how much of the course content you already knew. You are now half-way through the book! Now is the time to take the Mid-Quiz to see much you much you have learned. <u>Please DO NOT use any resources to complete this page</u>.

Match the roots to their meaning:	D2		
guard, keep	_____	א.ה.ב	A
to be wise	_____	שׁ.מ.ר	B
love	_____	ח.כ.ם	C
create, shape	_____	ב.ר.א	D
hear	_____	שׁ.מ.ע	E
live	_____	י.ר.ה	F
speak, word, thing	_____	ח.י.ה	G
hit the mark	_____	ד.ב.ר	H

Match the words to their meaning:	D1		
I	_____	לֶחֶם	A
you (fs)	_____	דָּבָר	B
king	_____	חָכְמָה	C
you (ms)	_____	אַתָּה	D
appointed time	_____	אֲנִי	E
he	_____	אֶרֶץ	F
wisdom	_____	כֹּל	G
heaven/s	_____	הוּא	H
word/thing	_____	שָׁמַיִם	I
all	_____	מֶלֶךְ	J
bread	_____	מִצְוָה	K
land/earth	_____	מוֹעֵד	L
commandment	_____	אַתְּ	M
son	_____	בֵּן	N

Match the prefixes to their meaning:	D3		
to/for	_____	הַ..	A
from	_____	בְּ..	B
in the/with the	_____	לְ..	C
the	_____	וְ..	D
and	_____	מִ..	E
in/with	_____	בַּ..	F

Translate the sentences into English:		
	אַתָּה הַמֶּלֶךְ.	D4
	בָּרָא אֱלֹהִים אֵת הַשָּׁמַיִם.	D5
	אֲנַחְנוּ מִיִשְׂרָאֵל.	D6
	בָּרוּךְ הַמִּצְוֹת!	D7

Answers are on the bottom of Appendix A, page 120.

Lesson 6 – Verbs

Hebrew Prayer "I love You, LORD"
אֲנִי אוֹהֵב אוֹתְךָ יְהוָה. man writing
אֲנִי אוֹהֶבֶת אוֹתְךָ יְהוָה. woman writing

A - Vocabulary

Memorize the following words:

English	*Gender*	Transliteration	Hebrew	
give (verb)	*ms*	*no-TEN*	נוֹתֵן	A1
love (verb)	*ms*	*o-HEV*	אוֹהֵב	A2
she, it	*fs*	*hee*	הִיא	A3
they	*mpl* *fpl*	*hem* *hen*	הֵם הֵן	A4

B – Verbs

In English, verbs (action words) change their endings based on who is doing the action. For example, "I love," "he loves," "she loves," "they love." In Hebrew, this is also true. B1

In *Hebrew with Joy! Book 1*, we introduced the word for "love" as a <u>noun</u>: אַהֲבָה from the root א.ה.ב. Here are the present tense <u>verb</u> endings for א.ה.ב: B2

א.ה.ב	ending	gender/ number	
אוֹהֵב	no ending	ms	B3
אוֹהֶבֶת	..ת	fs	B4
אוֹהֲבִים	..ִים	mpl (or mixed groups)	B5
אוֹהֲבוֹת	..וֹת	fpl	B6

Do you notice that the verb endings are like the noun endings in Lesson 5? The verb endings must match the gender (m or f) and number (s or pl) of the noun doing the action. <u>This verb group is one of several found in both Biblical and Modern Hebrew and is being taught as an introduction to the verbs used in Biblical Hebrew!</u> B7

Read and translate the following phrases: B8

הִיא אוֹהֶבֶת   הֵם אוֹהֲבִים   אַתָּה אוֹהֵב   הֵן אוֹהֲבוֹת

It is interesting to note that the phrases above can have several meanings! B9
For example הִיא אוֹהֶבֶת can mean "she loves" OR "she is one who loves" OR "she is loving."

C – Root - נ.ת.ן

Write the missing English word below:

give	נ.ת.ן 2008X	C1
(ms)	נוֹתֵן	C2
give/giver (fs)	נוֹתֶנֶת	C3
give/givers (mpl)	נוֹתְנִים	C4
give/givers (fpl)	נוֹתְנוֹת	C5
Jonathan (God gave)	יוֹנָתָן	C6
gift	מַתָּנָה	C7

Did you notice the similar verb endings in the roots א.ה.ב and נ.ת.ן? Again, these verbs are in the present tense, and belong to the same verb group. C8

Write the missing Hebrew for the following English phrases: C9

they (fpl) give   he gives   she gives   we give

D – Verb Chart

Here is a summary chart of the verbs and pronouns used in this lesson. D1
Fill in the missing root meanings in the first column on the right:

fpl	mpl	fs	ms		
הֵן אֲנַחְנוּ	הֵם אֲנַחְנוּ	אַתְּ אֲנִי הִיא	אַתָּה אֲנִי הוּא	pronouns	D2
▢וֹ▢ְ▢וֹת	▢וֹ▢ְ▢ִים	▢וֹ▢ֶ▢ֶת	▢וֹ▢ֵ▢	root	D3
נוֹתְנוֹת	נוֹתְנִים	נוֹתֶנֶת	נוֹתֵן	נ.ת.ן 	D4
שׁוֹמְרוֹת	שׁוֹמְרִים	שׁוֹמֶרֶת	שׁוֹמֵר	שׁ.מ.ר 	D5
אוֹהֲבוֹת	אוֹהֲבִים	אוֹהֶבֶת	אוֹהֵב	א.ה.ב 	D6

In each of the sentences below, circle the correct form of the Hebrew verb:

הִיא (נוֹתֵן נוֹתֶנֶת נוֹתְנִים נוֹתְנוֹת) אֶת הַתּוֹרָה. D7

הֵן (אוֹהֵב אוֹהֶבֶת אוֹהֲבִים אוֹהֲבוֹת) אֶת יִשְׂרָאֵל. D8

אֲנַחְנוּ (שׁוֹמֵר שׁוֹמֶרֶת שׁוֹמְרִים) אֶת הַמֶּלֶךְ. D9

E – I Love "You" LORD

To write "I love <u>you</u>, LORD" in Hebrew, the direct object "you" (ms) is the word **אוֹתְךָ.** E1

man writing **אֲנִי אוֹהֵב אוֹתְךָ יְהוָה.**

woman writing **אֲנִי אוֹהֶבֶת אוֹתְךָ יְהוָה.**

Depending on whether you are a man or a woman, E2
write "I love you, LORD" in Hebrew as a prayer to Adonai:

____

Note – The direct object "you" (fs), is the word is אוֹתָךְ.

F – Blessing the Giver of the Torah

F1

פָּרָשָׁה

In Jewish culture, the תּוֹרָה refers to the first five books of the Hebrew Bible. At the end of סֻכּוֹת (Feast of Tabernacles), the תּוֹרָה scroll reading for the previous year is completed (end of Deuteronomy) and the scroll is rolled back to the beginning (Genesis 1:1). Then, the first פָּרָשָׁה (Torah portion) is read. Traditionally, the Torah is divided into 54 פָּרָשׁוֹת (portion), and every Shabbat, Jews worldwide are all reading the same פָּרָשָׁה!

Complete this beautiful prayer that is recited before and after reading the פָּרָשָׁה (Torah portion) during Shabbat services:

הַתּוֹרָה.	נוֹתֵן	יְהוָה	אַתָּה	בָּרוּךְ	תְּפִילָה	F2
					Prayer	

The prayer above is the last line of the blessing before reading the פָּרָשָׁה. F3
Practice reading and <u>circle the two words with the root for "give</u>."

בָּרְכוּ אֶת יְיָ הַמְּבֹרָךְ.
בָּרוּךְ יְיָ הַמְּבֹרָךְ לְעוֹלָם וָעֶד.
בָּרוּךְ אַתָּה יְיָ אֱלֹהֵינוּ מֶלֶךְ הָעוֹלָם,
אֲשֶׁר בָּחַר בָּנוּ מִכָּל הָעַמִּים
וְנָתַן לָנוּ אֶת תּוֹרָתוֹ:
בָּרוּךְ אַתָּה יְיָ, נוֹתֵן הַתּוֹרָה. אָמֵן

Leader - Bless the LORD, the Blessed One. F4
All - Blessed is the LORD, the Blessed One, throughout all time.
Leader - Blessed are you, LORD our God, King of the universe,
Who has chosen us from among all peoples
And has given us His Instruction.
All - Blessed are You, LORD, giver of the Instruction. Amen

G – Technology – Pealim.com

When I am trying to dig deeper into a Hebrew verb to understand who is doing the action, I use a free website called **Pealim.com** ("verbs"). This program is also helpful when you write your own prayers and want to use the correct form of a verb. Type in an English verb (i.e. "give"), and the web page will give all forms of the Hebrew verb. Notice the present tense verbs in G2. G1

G2

Singular		Plural	
Masculine	Feminine	Masculine	Feminine
נוֹתֵן noten I / you *m. sg.* / he / it **give(s)**	נוֹתֶנֶת notenet I / you *f. sg.* / she / it **give(s)**	נוֹתְנִים notnim we / you *m. pl.* / they *m.* **give**	נוֹתְנוֹת notnot we / you *f. pl.* / they *f.* **give**

G3

Here are the steps to use Pealim.com:

1. Open **Pealim.com** on your computer (There is also a paid phone app).
2. Click on the **Toggle Hebrew keyboard** button

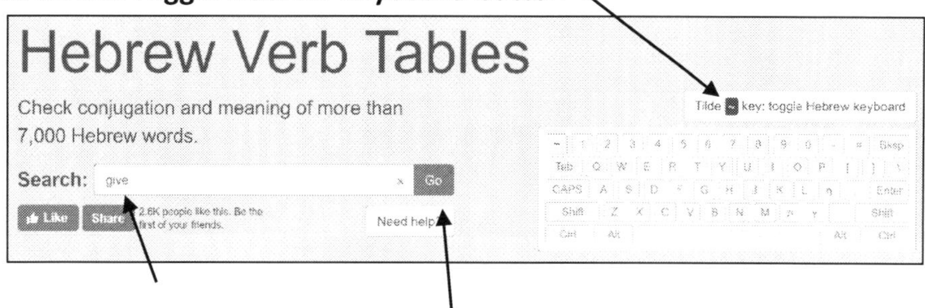

3. Type in a verb in English, then click **Go.**
4. Locate the line with the correct verb root, then click on the far-left word.

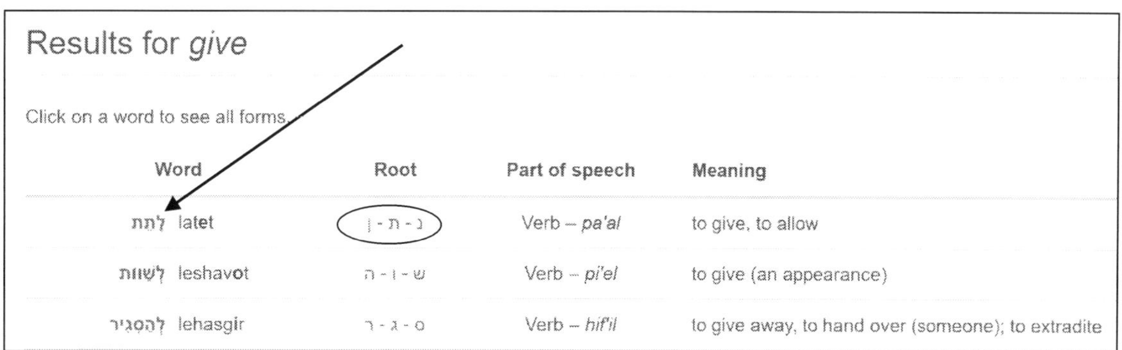

Results for *give*

Click on a word to see all forms.

Word	Root	Part of speech	Meaning
לָתֵת latet	נ - ת - ן	Verb – *pa'al*	to give, to allow
לְשַׁוּוֹת leshavot	ש - ו - ה	Verb – *pi'el*	to give (an appearance)
לְהַסְגִּיר lehasgir	ס - ג - ר	Verb – *hif'il*	to give away, to hand over (someone); to extradite

5. You may need to select the correct verb root again, then view the results (see G2 above).

Match the Pronouns and the Verbs!

Team Game: Photocopy two copies of this page, or download and print 2 copies from: https://hebrewwithjoy.com/bhj-handouts/ Cut out the pieces. Divide the students into 2 teams and give each team a complete set. The teams turn the pieces face down on a table. On a signal from the leader, teams turn over all of the pieces and try to match each noun with the matching verb separating the pairs into four piles: ms, fs, mpl and fpl. First team to match and separate all 12 sets wins the game. (There are many possible combinations.) **Individual Students:** Cut out the pieces, then match the 12 sets and read them.

אוֹהֲבוֹת	אֲנִי	אוֹהֵב
נוֹתְנִים	הֵן	אוֹהֶבֶת
הִיא	שׁוֹמֵר	אוֹהֲבִים
אֲנִי	שׁוֹמֶרֶת	הוּא
הֵן	שׁוֹמְרִים	הֵם
נוֹתֶנֶת	שׁוֹמְרוֹת	אֲנַחְנוּ
אַתְּ	הֵם	אַתָּה
נוֹתְנוֹת	נוֹתֵן	הֵן

שֵׁם______________ Lesson 6 Homework

In each of the sentences below, write the correct form of the missing Hebrew verb: .1

A הֵן ______________ אֶת הַתּוֹרָה.
(give)

B הִיא ______________ אֶת יִשְׂרָאֵל.
(love)

C יְהוָה ______________ אֶת הַמֶּלֶךְ.
(guard)

D אֲנַחְנוּ ______________ אֶת הָאָרֶץ.
(give)

Translate the following sentences: .2

	אַתְּ אוֹהֶבֶת אֶת יִשְׂרָאֵל.	A
	הִיא נוֹתֶנֶת אֶת הַתּוֹרָה.	B
	הֵן שׁוֹמְרוֹת אֶת הַמִּצְוֹת.	C
	אֲנִי אוֹהֵב אֶת הַמּוֹעֲדִים.	D
	הוּא נוֹתֵן חָכְמָה.	E
	אֲנַחְנוּ נוֹתְנִים לֶאֱלֹהִים.	F

Write three Hebrew words that come from the root נ.ת.ן and their English meanings: .3

______________ ______________ ______________

______________ ______________ ______________

Refer to Section E, and write a Hebrew prayer to Adonai, including "I love you LORD…" .4

____Hebrew

____

____

____English

____

____

In the Lessons 2 and 3 homework, you were challenged to select and memorize a .5
Scripture in Hebrew. Take time right now to practice it and begin to memorize it.

English Book and Verse: ______________________________

Hebrew Book and Verse: ______________________________

Extra Technology Challenge

Use **Pealim.com** to look up the verb "pray." Be sure to select the verb root פ.ל.ל. .6

How do you write "I (ms) pray" in Hebrew? .7

____________________ __________

How do you write "I (fs) pray" in Hebrew? .8

____________________ __________

Lesson 7 – Word Pairs

Hebrew Holiday Greeting
Holiday of Joy! !חַג שָׂמֵחַ

A - Vocabulary

Memorize the following words:

English	*Gender*	Transliteration	Hebrew	
covenant	*fs*	*b-REET*	בְּרִית	A1
forever/eternity/world/universe	*ms*	*o-LAM*	עוֹלָם	A2
house	*ms*	***BA**-yeet*	בַּיִת	A3
community/congregation	*fs*	*k-hee-LA*	קְהִילָּה	A4
joy (belonging to the LORD)	*fs*	*khed-VA*	חֶדְוָה	A5

B – Word Pairs - סְמִיכוּת

In English, we often put two nouns together to make a new single concept. Examples are "goldfish," "seat belt," and "water fountain." B1

Hebrew also uses word pairs which are called סְמִיכוּת (smee-KHOOT). B2

Examples: שַׁבַּת שָׁלוֹם Sabbath **of** peace אֶרֶץ יִשְׂרָאֵל land **of** Israel B3

Notice that in most word pairs, the word "**of**" must be added to translate correctly. B4

B5

שַׁבַּת שָׁלוֹם

As we learned in *Hebrew with Joy!,* the root of שַׁבָּת means "rest or stop," and the root of שָׁלוֹם means "completion or wholeness." Putting this word pair together reveals a blessing for complete wholeness (physical, spiritual, and emotional) which results from choosing to rest and stop from our normal busy life. In fact, when a Jewish woman lights the Shabbat candles, three times her hands circle the candles. This is a picture of pushing away the ordinary tasks and drawing in the sweet shalom of the Shabbat.

Read the following word pairs, then write the English meaning:

	בְּרִית עוֹלָם	B6
	שׁוֹמֵר הַתּוֹרָה	B7
	מֶלֶךְ הָעוֹלָם	B8
son of the ___________________	בַּר מִצְוָה	B9
tree **of** ___________	עֵץ חַיִּים	B10
_______ **of** Atonement	יוֹם כִּפּוּר	B11
head **of** the _______	רֹאשׁ הַשָּׁנָה	B12
__________ **of** blasting	יוֹם תְּרוּעָה	B13

B14

Rosh Hashana vs Yom T'ruah

Jews worldwide celebrate רֹאשׁ הַשָּׁנָה "Rosh Hashanah," the Jewish New Year, as the beginning of a new civil calendar year. רֹאשׁ הַשָּׁנָה is also celebrated as the first of the fall מוֹעֲדִים and the beginning of the "High Holy Days." Surprisingly, רֹאשׁ הַשָּׁנָה is not found in the Scriptures! Instead, the name of the holiday is יוֹם תְּרוּעָה "yom t-roo-A," the shouting or blasting of the trumpets.
In Numbers 29:1 we read, *"In the seventh month, on the first day of the month, you shall have a holy convocation; you shall do no work; it is a day for you to blast the trumpets."*

C – Word Pair Suffix Changes

At times, the vowels may change in the first word of a word pair. C1
For example, בַּיִת (house) changes to בֵּית (house of).

If the first word ends in ◌ִים.. (mpl) the ending changes to ◌ֵי.. C2
For example, בָּנִים (sons) changes to בְּנֵי (sons of).

Read the following word pairs, then write the English meaning below each pair: C3

בְּנֵי יִשְׂרָאֵל	אֱלֹהֵי אַבְרָהָם	בֵּית לֶחֶם
____________	____________	____________
____________	Abraham	____________

If the first word ends in ָה.. the ending changes to ַת.. C4

Here are two examples for "joy": שִׂמְחָה (joy) changes to שִׂמְחַת (joy of).
חֶדְוָה (joy) changes to חֶדְוַת (joy of).

Read the following word pairs, then write the English meaning below each pair: C5

חֶדְוַת יְהוָה	שִׂמְחַת תּוֹרָה	קְהִילַּת שָׁלוֹם
________	________	________
________	________	________

Where do we find our strength? Complete the Scripture to find out: C6

נְחֶמְיָה 8:10	כִּֽי־	חֶדְוַ֥ת	יְהוָ֖ה	הִ֥יא	מָֽעֻזְּכֶֽם.
________ 8:10	for				your (mpl) strength
Normal English					

*This precious Scripture is inscribed inside my husband's (Russ) wedding ring!

D – Root – צ.ו.ה

Write the missing English words below:

D1	צ.ו.ה 181X	command, order
D2	מִצְוָה	
D3	מִצְוֹת	
D4	בַּר מִצְוָה	son of the commandment
D5	בַּת מִצְוָה	daughter of the commandment

E – Attributes of GOD

E1

Meditate on יְהוָה

What is Biblical meditation? It challenges us to fill our minds with the truth of Adonai's Word and to ask the רוּחַ יְהוָה to enlighten our minds to understand those truths. When we meditate on Scripture, we exchange our feeble thoughts about who we think יְהוָה is for how He sees Himself (which is a perfect perspective).

The name of the LORD is a strong tower; the righteous run to it and are safe.

Proverbs 18:10 (From *Behold Your God* by Greg Wiley)

Many of the names used in the Tanakh that describe Adonai are word pairs. Practice reading and meditating on the names, then fill in the blanks in the following chart:

Scripture	English Meaning	Hebrew	
Ex. 3:15		אֱלֹהֵי אַבְרָהָם	E2
Zeph. 3:15		מֶלֶךְ יִשְׂרָאֵל	E3
Isa. 9:6	prince _____ ____________	שַׂר־שָׁלוֹם	E4
Judges 6:24		יְהוָה שָׁלוֹם	E5
Isa. 11:2	spirit _____ __________	רוּחַ חָכְמָה	E6
Deut. 10:17		אֱלֹהֵי הָאֱלֹהִים	E7
Isa. 43:15		בּוֹרֵא יִשְׂרָאֵל	E8

F – Technology – Hebrew-English Dictionaries

As you become more interested in Hebrew, you will want to see the meaning of individual Hebrew words. There are many online Hebrew-English dictionaries that can help you. Remember that apps are continually changing, so always check for newer versions.

At the time of publishing, my favorite iPhone app is **Hebrew Dictionary 18A5** by Prolog. (Different versions are available for Android phones.) Although this app has a free version, for a small one-time charge, you have access to the entire dictionary.

The app includes the vowels, accented syllables, and gender for each word. It also shows related words and phrases. The example below requires the paid version.

1: Download the **Hebrew Dictionary 18A5** app on your cell phone.

2: Type in an English word, then select the specific word from the list by clicking the plus sign.

3: Notice the Hebrew spelling, the vowels and the accented syllable. Also notice the gender: [נ] feminine or [ז] masculine.

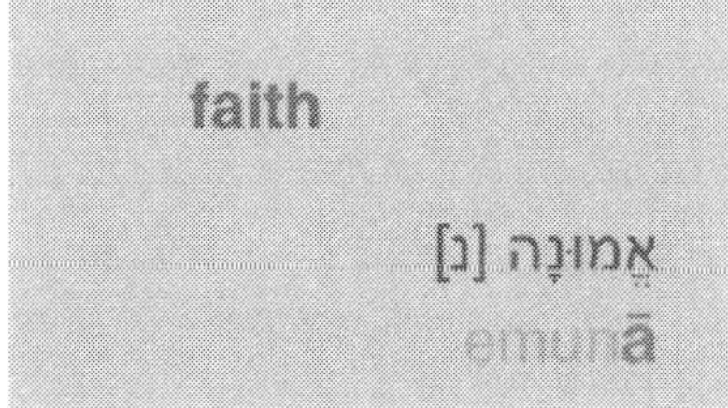

Find the סְמִיכוּת Word Pairs

In this puzzle, circle the Hebrew letters for the word pairs numbered below. (They may be horizontal, vertical or diagonal.) If you are a part of a group, work in teams to see which team can find all the word pairs in the least amount of time. Note that there are no spaces between the two Hebrew words in each word pair.

1. House of Bread 2. Day of Atonement 3. King of the universe 4. Joy of Torah 5. Joy of the LORD 6. Sons/Children of Israel 7. God of Abraham 8. Covenant of eternity 9. Congregation of Peace

ע	כ	א	ת	פ	מ	נ	א	ב	ל	ל	ט	ף	ג	צ
ל	ר	ז	נ	ץ	כ	ש	ל	ש	ר	א	ב	ק	מ	נ
ק	ן	ב	ס	ק	צ	ש	ר	ם	נ	ר	ר	ץ	א	ל
ה	ר	ו	ת	ת	ח	מ	ש	ק	ש	ש	י	ג	ס	מ
י	א	ל	מ	ב	מ	מ	ה	ו	ה	י	ת	ו	ד	ח
ל	פ	ד	ם	ח	ל	ת	י	ב	כ	י	ע	ט	ס	כ
ת	ו	א	ץ	ל	ד	פ	נ	כ	ל	נ	ו	ך	י	ל
ש	פ	ב	ל	צ	ה	ו	ב	ס	ב	ב	ל	ו	ך	ב
ל	נ	ת	ש	ש	ע	ת	א	ש	ו	צ	ם	ש	ד	ב
ו	מ	ת	ב	נ	ו	ק	ס	ר	ל	כ	ז	מ	ה	ר
ם	ז	ק	ח	ב	ל	נ	ש	ד	פ	ץ	פ	צ	ב	א
מ	כ	ג	ד	ר	ם	ה	א	ו	ש	ה	כ	ס	נ	ו
ס	ס	נ	צ	ל	ם	ה	ר	ב	א	י	ה	ל	א	ת

Lesson 7 Homework

שֵׁם______________

1. Write the matching letter to make a word pair. Each letter should be used only once:

A	אֶרֶץ	____	אֵל
B	בֵּית	____	תּוֹרָה
C	יוֹם	____	יִשְׂרָאֵל
D	קְהִילַּת	____	שָׁלוֹם
E	מֶלֶךְ	____	שָׂמֵחַ
F	אֱלֹהֵי	____	כִּפּוּר
G	חַג	____	הָעוֹלָם
H	שִׂמְחַת	____	אַבְרָהָם

2. Translate the following phrases into normal English sentences. (Don't forget to include words such as "is," "am," "are," "of"):

A	בָּרוּךְ בְּנֵי יִשְׂרָאֵל.	
B	הוּא מֶלֶךְ הָעוֹלָם.	
C	אֲנַחְנוּ אוֹהֲבִים אֶת קְהִילַּת שָׁלוֹם.	
D	אַתְּ אוֹהֶבֶת אֶת בֵּית אֵל.	
E	הִיא שׁוֹמֶרֶת אֶת הַמִּצְוֹת.	
F	בָּרָא יְהוָה אֶת אֶרֶץ יִשְׂרָאֵל.	
G	הֵן נוֹתְנוֹת אֶת הַתּוֹרָה.	

3. In a Hebrew word pair, what word is often added when translating to English? ___________

4. What is the root meaning of צ.ו.ה? ________________

5. Write two Hebrew words that come from this root and their English meanings:

____________E ______________H ______________E _______________H

How long is the Sabbath to be kept? Complete the Scripture to find out: .6

הַשַּׁבָּת	אֶת־	בְנֵי־ יִשְׂרָאֵל	וְשָׁמְרוּ	שְׁמוֹת 31:16
			______they will ___________	___________ 31:16

עוֹלָם׃	בְּרִית	לְדֹרֹתָם	הַשַּׁבָּת	אֶת־	לַעֲשׂוֹת
		_______ their generations			_____ make

	Normal English

Refer to sections D and E. Using the correct form of "love," .7
write a Hebrew and English prayer to Adonai.

Examples: אֲנִי אוֹהֶבֶת אֶת אֱלֹהֵי יִשְׂרָאֵל. (fs)

אֲנִי אוֹהֵב אֶת אֱלֹהֵי יִשְׂרָאֵל. (ms)

______________________________ Hebrew

____

______________________________ English

____

Using a Hebrew-English dictionary, look up the Hebrew word for "joy." .8
(You'll find many different words!) Write 4 of the Hebrew words below:

______________ ______________

______________ ______________

Lesson 8 – The Priestly Blessing

Hebrew Greeting

Good morning! !בּוֹקֶר טוֹב A.

Morning light! !בּוֹקֶר אוֹר B.

A - Vocabulary

Memorize the following words:

English	Gender	Transliteration	Hebrew	
grace	*ms*	*khen*	חֵן	A1
toward you	*ms*	*e-**LE**-kha*	אֵלֶיךָ	A2
light/shine	*ms*	*or*	אוֹר	A3
to you	*ms, mpl*	*l-KHA, l-KHEM*	לְךָ,לָכֶם	A4
his face*	*ms*	*pa-NAV*	פָּנָיו	A5

*More on פָּנָיו in lesson 9

B – Pronoun Suffixes ךָ.. and כֶם.. "you/your"

In English, when we want to show possession (what belongs to you) we use pronouns like "your..." as in "your peace." In Biblical Hebrew, both words are combined into one! B1

The suffix ךָ.. adds "your" or "you" (ms) to a word.

Examples: שָׁלוֹם (peace) changes to שְׁלוֹמְךָ (your peace- ms) B2

..לְ (to) changes to לְךָ (to you - ms)

The suffix כֶם.. adds "your" or "you" (mpl) to a word. B3

Examples: אֱלֹהִים (God) changes to אֱלֹהֵיכֶם (your God - mpl)

..לְ (to) changes to לָכֶם (to you - mpl)

If the word ends in a ה, a ת is added and the ה drops. B4

Example: תּוֹרָה changes to תּוֹרָתְךָ "your instruction."

Read and translate the following words and be sure to include "you" or "your": B5

לְךָ אֱלֹהֵיכֶם לָכֶם תּוֹרָתְךָ שְׁלוֹמְךָ

____ ________ ________ ________ ________

____ ________ ________ ________ ________

C – Future Action Prefix – "..י"

Many of the words in the Aaronic Blessing start with a "י" C1
Often, the "י" is a prefix which indicates a future action. Examples:

ךָ + בָרֶכְ + יְ = יְבָרֶכְךָ = "**will** bless you"
you bless will

ךָ + שְׁמְרֶ + יִ + וְ = וְיִשְׁמְרֶךָ = "and **will** keep you."
you keep will and

In the Aaronic Blessing below, notice that the "י" in יְהוָה is not a prefix. C2
Also notice that cantillation marks have been included to help you get familiar with them in your Hebrew Bibles. <u>Circle the letter "י" where it is used as a prefix</u> in the Aaronic Blessing:

יְבָרֶכְךָ֥ יְהוָ֖ה וְיִשְׁמְרֶֽךָ׃
יָאֵ֨ר יְהוָ֧ה ׀ פָּנָ֛יו אֵלֶ֖יךָ וִֽיחֻנֶּֽךָּ׃
יִשָּׂ֨א יְהוָ֤ה ׀ פָּנָיו֙ אֵלֶ֔יךָ וְיָשֵׂ֥ם לְךָ֖ שָׁלֽוֹם׃

D – Root - ח.נ.ן

The key to understanding the meaning of a complex Hebrew word is first to look for the root and translate, then to translate the prefixes and suffixes that have been added to the root. D1

Notice the following new root that is used in the Aaronic Blessing. Can you see how it forms the building blocks for more complex words? D2

Write the missing English word below:

Word meaning	Hebrew Word		Meaning of Root	Root	
ךָּ + חֻנֶּ + י + וִ (to) you be gracious will and	וִיחֻנֶּךָּ	D4	**grace, mercy, favor**	ח.נ.ן 78X	D3
	חֵן	D5			
Hannah	חַנָּה	D6			

E– Aaronic Blessing

E1

בִּרְכַּת הַכֹּהֲנִים

Because of the simple and beautiful words expressed in the Aaronic Blessing (*beer-KAT ha-ko-ha-NEEM* – Blessing of the Priests), it has been spoken since ancient times. Today in Judaism it is known as the Priestly Blessing, the Priestly Benediction, the Beautiful Blessing or the "Raising of the Hands." Adonai clearly reminds us of the importance of this prayer: *"In this way, they* [the priests] *are to place My Name over Bnei-Yisrael, and so I will bless them."* Numbers 6:27

Speaking this Aaronic blessing over a loved one can be life-changing! Read the Scripture aloud. The cantillation marks will help you to accent the correct syllable. Then, complete the charts below (most of the fill-in words are from your vocabulary and root lists but include prefixes and suffixes): E2

E3

וְיִשְׁמְרֶךָ׃		יְבָרֶכְךָ	בְּמִדְבַּר 6:24-26
	LORD		________ 6:24-26
			Normal English

E4

וִיחֻנֶּךָּ׃	אֵלֶיךָ	פָּנָיו		יָאֵר
			LORD	will shine
				Normal English

E5

שָׁלוֹם׃	לְךָ	וְיָשֵׂם	אֵלֶיךָ	פָּנָיו		יִשָּׂא
		________ will put			LORD	will lift up
						Normal English

F – Hannah Nesher - Aaronic Blessing

For many years, my husband and I have had the privilege of studying each week's Parashah F1
(Torah portion) with Hannah Nesher, using her insightful studies on her Voiceforlsrael.net website. The following excerpts are from Parashat "Naso" and have been used with her permission.

1. "**The Lord יהוה bless you"**...The first element of the blessing requires **humility.** Blessing (y-va-REKH) יְבָרֵךְ contains the same root as knee **BE**-rekh **בֶּרֶךְ.** It takes real humility - getting down on our knees (figuratively or literally) - to receive the blessing of God.

2. "**and keep you....**" The word for "keep" is shomer שׁוֹמֵר which means "to *guard, watch over, and protect from all evil, sickness, poverty and calamity."*

3. **"Adonai make His face to shine upon you...**" God's face shining upon us denotes His attention, favor, light and friendship.

4. **"and be gracious unto you..."**
If we seek the face of God, instead of just His hands – what He can give us – He can cause His favor and grace to be poured out upon us. The word used here in Hebrew comes from the root חֵן (khen) meaning "grace" (which is also the root of Hannah's name!).

5. **"Adonai lift up His face upon you..."**
Here, the word for "lift up" יִשָּׂא (yisah) comes from the same root as Naso, the title of this parashah. It means 'to elevate.' Most translations write, 'His countenance;' but actually the Hebrew word used is the same as in the previous verse – "panav" – His face. It means God turns His attention toward you.

6. **And give you peace (shalom)....**
The pinnacle of this blessing is for "shalom" שָׁלוֹם peace. "Give" would be "yee-ten," but the word used here is יָשֵׂם "ya-SEM." "La-seem" (the root) is to "set, place, or establish." It is not just that the Lord "gives" us peace, He actually "sets, places, and establishes us in a place of shalom."

F2

The Priestly Hands

While pronouncing the blessing, the Kohen would spread his fingers apart, placing his thumbs together to represent the Hebrew letter Sheen. Sheen is also the letter on the mezuzah and stands for El Shaddai, God Almighty. According to Jewish tradition, the divine presence would shine through the fingers of the High Priest as he blessed the people. Therefore, no one was allowed to look at him during the blessing, out of respect and awe of the power of the Almighty.

(Jewish Jewels Newsletter, Aug. 2018 www.jewishjewels.org)

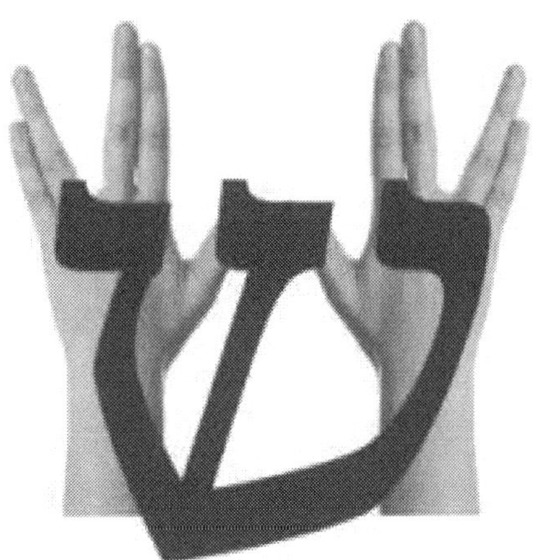

G – Technology – YouTube Videos & iTunes

We can all agree that memorizing Scripture can be very challenging. For many people, adding music makes this process a lot easier.

If you have a great love for music, you have most likely discovered both **YouTube** and **iTunes**. You can explore thousands of songs and lyrics with just the click of a button.

Take a moment to open either **YouTube** or **iTunes** and search for "Aaronic Blessing." Then, while the video or music is playing, read along with the Hebrew below.

יְבָרֶכְךָ יְהוָה וְיִשְׁמְרֶךָ׃

יָאֵר יְהוָה פָּנָיו אֵלֶיךָ וִיחֻנֶּךָּ׃

יִשָּׂא יְהוָה פָּנָיו אֵלֶיךָ וְיָשֵׂם לְךָ שָׁלוֹם׃

Aaronic Blessing Board Game

Each player or team places a unique marker on Start. Roll a die and move forward the number on the die. Each time you land on a word, read it and translate. The first player or team to reach the end wins.
Download at https://hebrewwithjoy.com/bhj-handouts/

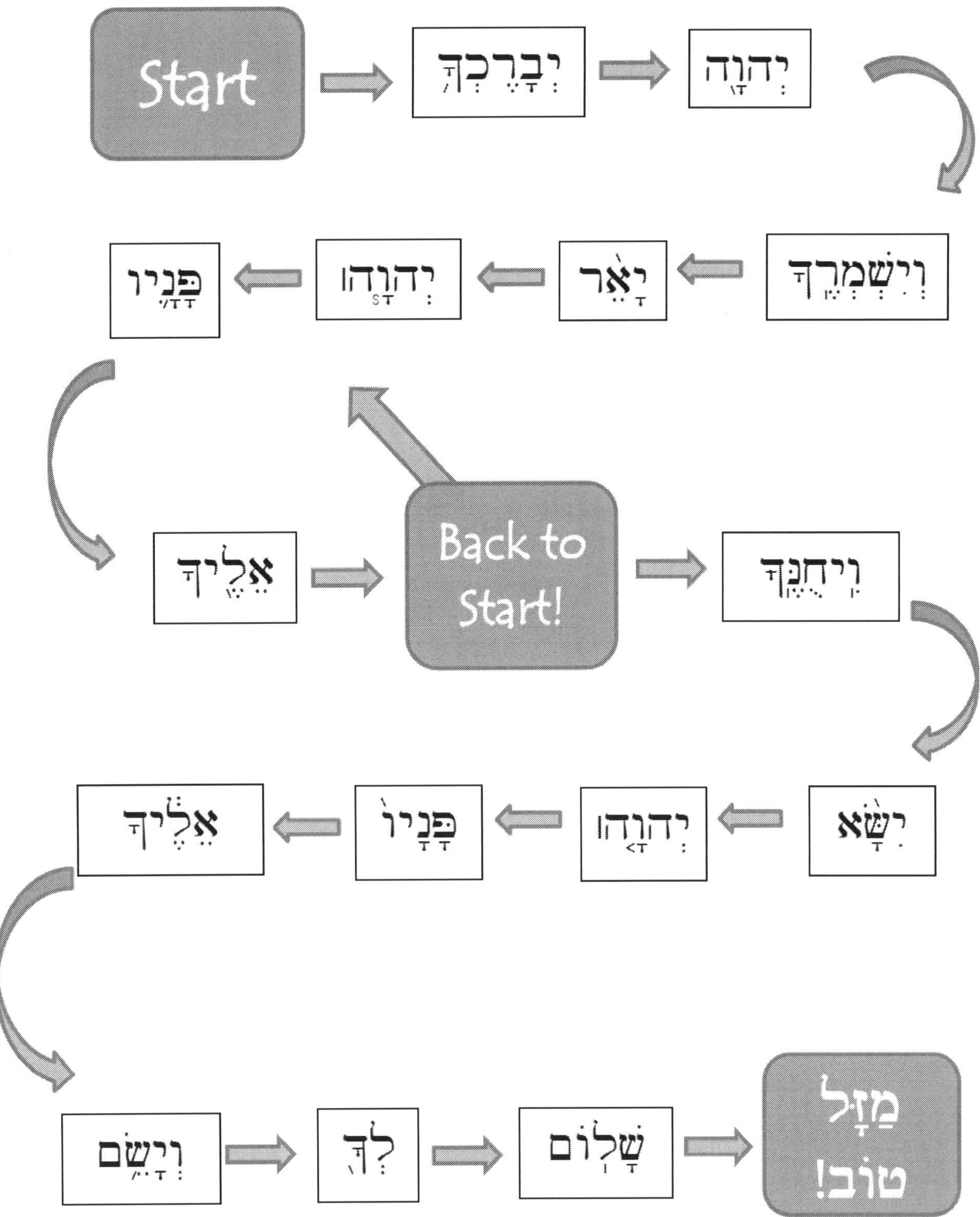

שֵׁם ______________ Lesson 8 Homework

Complete the chart below to discover a precious promise from Adonai. Remember to include the translation of the prefixes and suffixes as separate words: .1

אֶת־נַפְשֶׁךָ	יִשְׁמֹר	רָע	מִכָּל־	יִשְׁמָרְךָ		תְּהִלִּים 121:7
________ soul		evil			LORD	________ 121:7
						Normal English

What are two meanings of the suffixes ..כֶם & ..ךָ? _______ ________ .2

In the two words that start with "י" above, what does the "י" represent? .3

Circle one: past action present action future action

Translate the following phrases into normal English sentences (adding the missing English words). Some of these are from the Aaronic Blessing:

	יָאֵר יְהוָה פָּנָיו אֵלֶיךָ.	.4
	יְהוָה מֶלֶךְ הָעוֹלָם.	.5
	אֲנִי שׁוֹמֵר אֵת הָאוֹר הָעוֹלָם.	.6
	שָׁלוֹם לָכֶם.	.7
	בָּרוּךְ בְּנֵי יִשְׂרָאֵל.	.8
	בָּרָא אֱלֹהִים אֵת הַשָּׁמַיִם.	.9
	יְבָרֶכְךָ יְהוָה.	.10

What is the root meaning of ח.נ.ן? ________________ .11

Write two Hebrew words that come from this root and their English meanings: .12

____________E ______________H ______________E ______________H

Match the roots to their meaning: .13

give		ב.ר.א	A
guard/keep		י.ר.ה	B
bless/kneel		נ.ת.ן	C
speak/word/thing		שׂ.מ.ח	D
to be wise		ח.י.ה	E
create		א.ה.ב	F
joyful		ב.ר.ך	G
command		ח.נ.ן	H
hit the mark		צ.ו.ה	I
love		ח.כ.ם	J
live		שׁ.מ.ר	K
grace, mercy, favor		ד.ב.ר	L

Using **iTunes** or **YouTube**, try to memorize the Aaronic Blessing by listening to it over and over. Read the Hebrew below while you listen: .14

יְבָרֶכְךָ֥ יְהוָ֖ה וְיִשְׁמְרֶֽךָ׃

יָאֵ֨ר יְהוָ֧ה ׀ פָּנָ֛יו אֵלֶ֖יךָ וִיחֻנֶּֽךָּ׃

יִשָּׂ֨א יְהוָ֤ה ׀ פָּנָיו֙ אֵלֶ֔יךָ וְיָשֵׂ֥ם לְךָ֖ שָׁלֽוֹם׃

Were you able to memorize the Aaronic blessing? __________ .15

What blessed you as you were learning it?

____

____

____

Lesson 9 – Pronoun Suffixes

אָבִינוּ מַלְכֵּנוּ, אַתָּה אֱלֹהֵינוּ!
Our Father, our King, You are our GOD!

A - Vocabulary

Memorize the following words:

English	*Gender*	Transliteration	Hebrew	
father	*ms*	*av*	אָב	A1
remember	*ms (verb)*	*zo-KHER*	זוֹכֵר	A2
his commandments	*fpl*	*meets-vo-TAV* *(refer to p51 D3)*	מִצְוֹתָיו	A3
our GOD	*ms*	*e-lo-**HAY**-noo*	אֱלֹהֵינוּ	A4

** The complete list of suffixes is in Appendix I, page 139

B – Pronoun Suffix ◌ִי.. "my"

The suffix ◌ִי.. adds "my" or occasionally "I" or "me" to a word. B1

Examples: אָב (father) changes to אָבִי (my father)

..לְ (to) changes to לִי (to me)

Remember that vowels and sometimes letters may change when the suffix is added. B2

Examples: בַּיִת (house) changes to בֵּיתִי (my house)

תּוֹרָה (instruction) changes to תּוֹרָתִי (my instruction)

Read and translate the following words, adding "my" or "me": B3

בֵּיתִי אָבִי שְׁמִי תּוֹרָתִי לִי

____ ____ ____ ____ ____

______ ______ ______ ______ ______

Why is the study of the Word of GOD so important? Complete the chart below: B4

לִנְתִיבָתִי׃	וְאוֹר	דְּבָרֶךָ	לְרַגְלִי	נֵר־	תְּהִלִּים 119:105
______ ______ path	______ ________	______ ________	______ ______ feet	lamp	________ 119:105
					Normal English

Psalm 119:105

The Hebrew word for **LIGHT** אוֹר, has depths of meaning that can be life-transforming. It conveys illumination, as in a bright clear day, but it also means the light of instruction. The Hebrew word for **LAMP** is נִיר or נֵר. His lamp (to our feet) shines where our feet are standing today and His **LIGHT** (to our paths) illuminates what's up ahead on the road, present and future! We need God's light in our lives, and Scripture tells us that His Word is both our lamp and our light! We also learn in Psalm 27:1 that … *"The Lord (Himself!) is my light and my salvation. Whom shall we fear?"* Psalm 119:130 *"the entrance of your Word brings light!"* (Deb Wiley, author of *Ears to Hear*) B5

C – Pronoun Suffix נוּ.. "our"

The suffix נוּ.. adds "our" or occasionally "we" or "us" to a word. C1

Example : מֶלֶךְ (king) changes to מַלְכֵּנוּ (our king)

Sometimes another letter is also added before the נוּ.. ending. C2

Examples: אָב (father) changes to אָבִינוּ (our father)

אֲנִי (I) changes to אֲנַחְנוּ (we) and ..לְ (to) changes to לָנוּ (to us)

If the word ends in ◌ִים.. the ם drops, and the vowels change. C3

Example: אֱלֹהִים (GOD) changes to אֱלֹהֵינוּ (our GOD)

Read and translate the following words, and include the word "our": C4

לָנוּ	אֲנַחְנוּ	תּוֹרָתֵינוּ	מַלְכֵּנוּ	אֱלֹהֵינוּ	אָבִינוּ
______	______	______	______	______	______
______		______	______	______	______

Can you translate the בְּרָכָה (the beginning phrase of most traditional blessings)? C5

הָעוֹלָם		אֱלֹהֵינוּ		אַתָּה		Hebrew
	king		LORD		blessed	English

Ancient אָב

What is a Father? In the original pictographic script for אָב , the א is the picture of an ox , which means strength. The ב is a picture of a tent or house , where a family resides. When combined, these letters form the meaning "strength of the house."
(Jeff A. Benner, *Ancient Hebrew Dictionary*)

C6

D – Pronoun Suffixes ָיו.. וֹ.. "his"

The suffix וֹ.. adds "his" or occasionally "him," "he" or "it" to a word. D1
Sometimes the vowels and letters will change:

Examples: שֵׁם (name) changes to שְׁמוֹ (his name)
..לְ (to) changes to לוֹ (to him)

If the word ends in ה, the ה drops and the ת is added. D2
Example: תּוֹרָה (instruction) changes to תּוֹרָתוֹ (his instruction).

If the original word has a plural ending, a "י" may be added before the "ו". D3
This ָיו.. ending sounds like "av."
Examples: פָּנִים (face) changes to פָּנָיו (his face – pa-NAV)
מִצְוֹת (commandments) changes to מִצְוֹתָיו (his commandments)

Read and translate the following words and include the word "his," "him" or "it": D4

לְקַדְּשׁוֹ	פָּנָיו	מִצְוֹתָיו	תּוֹרָתוֹ	שְׁמוֹ	לוֹ
to holy ______	______	______	______	______	______
(to make it holy)	______	______	______	______	______

***In these last two lessons, we have studied the most common suffixes. D5
A complete list is included in Appendix I, page 139.

Review the pronoun suffixes by writing the English meaning for each Hebrew word: D6

לְךָ	מִצְוֹתָיו	מַלְכֵּנוּ	שְׁמִי	תּוֹרָתְךָ
____	____	____	____	____
____	____	____	____	____

אֱלֹהֵיכֶם	לוֹ	אֱלֹהֵינוּ	פָּנָיו	תּוֹרָתֵינוּ	D7
____	____	____	____	____	
____	____	____	____	____	

שְׁמוֹ	תּוֹרָתוֹ	לָנוּ	לִי	אָבִינוּ	D8
____	____	____	____	____	
____	____	____	____	____	

E - Root – ז.כ.ר

Fill in the missing English word and the gender and number (ms, fs, mpl or fpl):

remember	ז.כ.ר 233X	E1
( )	זוֹכֵר	E2
remember ( )	זוֹכֶרֶת	E3
remember ( )	זוֹכְרִים	E4
remember ( )	זוֹכְרוֹת	E5
Day of Remembrance (Memorial Day)	יוֹם הַזִּכָּרוֹן	E6
will remember (Memorial Prayer)	יִזְכֹּר	E7

 E8

What are we commanded to remember and do? E9

לְקַדְּשׁוֹ.	הַשַּׁבָּת	יוֹם	אֶת־	זָכוֹר	שְׁמוֹת 20:8
_____ (make) it _________					________ 20:8
					Normal English

E10

Remember!

Throughout the Tanakh, we are commanded to "remember" what Adonai has done. We see this in all of the מוֹעֲדִים, in the Ten Commandments (see E9 above), and in the altar stones that Adonai commanded to be built. During פֶּסַח, the children ask, "Why do we celebrate?" And the answer: "To remember the miracles that Adonai has done for us!"

Today in Israel, small stones of remembrance are placed on the gravestones of loved ones. On יוֹם הַזִּכָּרוֹן (the Day of Remembrance), Israelis grieve as they remember their fallen soldiers who have sacrificed their lives for their beloved country. Then, at sundown, all of Israel rejoices in יוֹם הָעַצְמָאוּת (Israeli Independence Day) as they remember the amazing freedom that Jewish people are now blessed with.

עַם יִשְׂרָאֵל חַי!

F – Technology – Bible Gateway

If you want to copy and paste your favorite Scriptures in Hebrew (including vowels and cantillation marks), then **Bible Gateway** is an amazing free tool to use! Here are the steps to use the program on your computer:

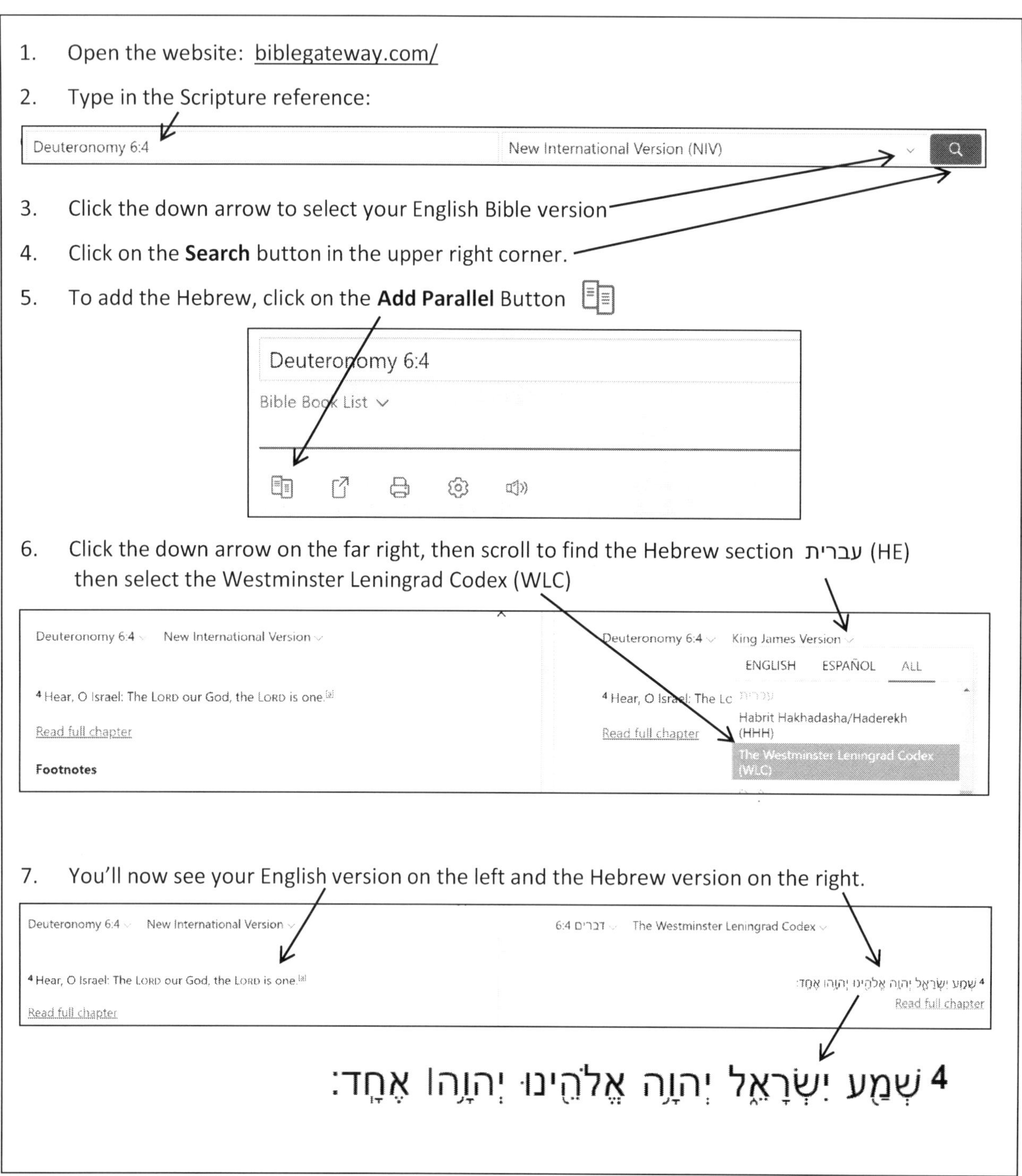

1. Open the website: biblegateway.com/
2. Type in the Scripture reference:
3. Click the down arrow to select your English Bible version
4. Click on the **Search** button in the upper right corner.
5. To add the Hebrew, click on the **Add Parallel** Button
6. Click the down arrow on the far right, then scroll to find the Hebrew section עברית (HE) then select the Westminster Leningrad Codex (WLC)
7. You'll now see your English version on the left and the Hebrew version on the right.

Prefix – Suffix Slap Game

If you are studying in a group, one person calls out the English meaning of a prefix or suffix (i.e. "prefix - from"); then, two other people try to be the first to **slap** that correct square (or say the square number). After using all the blocks, rotate so there is a new caller. If you are studying by yourself, read each block, and translate the meaning of the prefix or suffix.

3 ..וֹ	2 בְּ..	1 מִ..
6 וְ..	5 הַ..	4 ..נוּ
9 ..ךָ	8 לְ..	7 ..י
12 ..◌ָיו	11 ..כֶם	10 בַּ..

Prefixes: to/for, from, the, and,
in the/with the, in/with

Suffixes: my, your (ms), your (mpl),
his, our

שֵׁם___________ Lesson 9 Homework

In each box, match the Hebrew words to their English meaning: .1

our father		לְקַדְּשׁוֹ	A
my father		לִי	B
your father		אָבִיךָ	C
his commandments		לָכֶם	D
to make it holy		לוֹ	E
to him		לְךָ	F
to me		אָבִינוּ	G
to you (mpl)		אָבִי	H
to you (ms)		מִצְוֹתָיו	I

your instruction		תּוֹרָתִי	A
his instruction		תּוֹרָתוֹ	B
our instruction		אֱלֹהֵיכֶם	C
my instruction		אֱלֹהֵינוּ	D
his face		תּוֹרָתֵינוּ	E
my name		פָּנָיו	F
our God		תּוֹרָתְךָ	G
your (mpl) God		אֱלֹהֶיךָ	H
your (ms) God		שְׁמִי	I

Translate the following phrases into <u>complete</u> English sentences: .2

	אַתָּה אֱלֹהֵינוּ.	A
	אָבִי זוֹכֵר אֶת הַחָכְמָה מִתּוֹרָתְךָ.	B
	אֲנִי זוֹכֶרֶת אֶת שְׁמוֹ.	C
	אָבִינוּ מַלְכֵּנוּ, בָּרוּךְ אַתָּה.	D
	אֲנַחְנוּ שׁוֹמְרִים אֶת מַלְכֵּנוּ.	E
	הוּא זוֹכֵר אֶת בֵּיתִי.	F
	אֲנַחְנוּ שׁוֹמְרִים אֶת מִצְוֹתָיו.	G
	אֲנַחְנוּ זוֹכְרִים אֶת פָּנָיו.	H

What is the root meaning of ז.כ.ר? _______________ .3

Write two Hebrew words that come from this root and their English meanings: .4

____________E ___________H ____________E ____________H

In Lessons 2, 3 and 6, you were challenged to memorize a short Scripture in Hebrew (one that you did not already know in Hebrew). Your challenge is to finish memorizing it before you complete this course! .5

English Book and Verse: ______________________________

Hebrew Book and Verse: ______________________________

Write your Scripture in normal English: .6

____

____

____

Using a Hebrew Bible or any technology resource, write your Scripture in Hebrew in the charts below and translate each word into English: .7

					Hebrew
					English

					Hebrew
					English

					Hebrew
					English

In your Scripture above, carefully do the following: .8

Underline the prefixes that you have learned. .a

Double-Underline the suffixes that you have learned. .b

Circle the roots and words that you know. .c

Extra Technology Challenge

Use **Bible Gateway** to help you memorize your verse. Find your Scripture in Hebrew, then copy and paste it into your word processor. Make the font size bigger so that it is easy to read. Print out your Hebrew Scripture and display it in your home so you can practice reading it often. Use **Serve-A-Verse** to help you pronounce the words correctly. .9

Lesson 10 – Adjectives

Prayer for complete healing!
!רְפוּאָה שְׁלֵמָה

A - Vocabulary

Memorize the following words:

English	Gender	Transliteration	Hebrew	
big/great	ms	ga-DOL	גָּדוֹל	A1
good	ms	tov	טוֹב	A2
for/because	-	kee	כִּי	A3
work/serve/worship	ms	o-VED	עוֹבֵד	A4
heart	ms	lev/le-VAV	לֵב/לֵבָב	A5

טוֹב A6

"God saw that the light was טוֹב." Genesis 1:4

טוֹב first appears in the Scriptures when God proclaimed that the light was *good*. Many people see the light of God's truth and move towards it, but it seems there are so very few who behold how awesomely טוֹב that light is!

(*In His Own Words* by L. Grant Luton)

B – Adjectives

Adjectives are words that describe nouns. In both Biblical Hebrew and modern Hebrew, the adjective comes AFTER the noun. B1

Examples: a great king = מֶלֶךְ גָּדוֹל

a holy name = שֵׁם קָדוֹשׁ

The ending on the adjective must match the gender (m or f) and the number (s or pl) of the noun it describes. B2

Examples: a good congregation = קְהִילָּה טוֹבָה

big/great guards = שׁוֹמְרִים גְּדוֹלִים

Below is a summary of the adjective endings for “big/great” and “good” and “holy:”

holy	good	big/great	Gender Number	
קָדוֹשׁ	טוֹב	גָּדוֹל	ms	B3
קְדוֹשָׁה	טוֹבָה	גְּדוֹלָה	fs	B4
קְדוֹשִׁים	טוֹבִים	גְּדוֹלִים	mpl	B5
קְדוֹשׁוֹת	טוֹבוֹת	גְּדוֹלוֹת	fpl	B6

Read and translate the following phrases into English: B7

שׁוֹמְרִים טוֹבִים	קְהִילָּה גְּדוֹלָה	לֵב קָדוֹשׁ
____________	____________	____________
____________	____________	____________

Who is Adonai? Complete this entire Scripture to find out: B8

	גָּדוֹל	אֵל	כִּי	תְּהִלִּים 95:3
LORD				________ 95:3
				Normal English

אֱלֹהִים׃	כָּל־	עַל־	גָּדוֹל	וּמֶלֶךְ
		above		
				Normal English

If there is a "הַ" before the noun, the "הַ" must also come before the adjective. B9

Examples: the holy king = הַמֶּלֶךְ הַקָּדוֹשׁ

the good congregation = הַקְּהִילָּה הַטּוֹבָה

Write the Hebrew translation for the following phrases: B10

the good heart ______________ ______________

the great father ______________ ______________

B11

Hebrew Adjectives

In English, we say "I am a good person" or "I am a bad person." By putting the adjective (good or bad) before the noun (person), we tend to focus on the adjective. We judge ourselves and others too quickly. This is not how Adonai looks at us. He sees, in Hebrew, the person first, who is made in His image. He wants us to know how much He loves us and wants us to give our "adjectives," especially our issues and challenges, to Him.

(Excerpt from Jonathan Cahn *The Book of Mysteries* – Day 240)

C – Root – ע.ב.ד

Write the missing English word below:

work, serve, worship	ע.ב.ד 290x	C1
(verbs)	עוֹבֵד, עוֹבֶדֶת, עוֹבְדִים, עוֹבְדוֹת	C2
work/service (noun)	עֲבוֹדָה	C3
work! serve! worship! (command! mpl)	עִבְדוּ	C4
Obadiah (servant of God)	עֹבַדְיָה	C5
slave	עֶבֶד	C6

What was Joshua's promise regarding his family? Complete the chart below: C7

יְהוָה׃	אֶת־	נַעֲבֹד	וּבֵיתִי	וְאָנֹכִי	יְהוֹשֻׁעַ 24:15b
		will ________		______ me	
					Normal English

Who are we are commanded to serve, worship, and work for, and how should it be done? C8

בְּשִׂמְחָה.	יְהוָה	אֶת־	עִבְדוּ	תְּהִלִּים 100:2
______ ________				________ 100:2
				Normal English

Psalm 100:2

C9

This powerful verse has become a life verse for me. I encourage you to memorize it as a reminder that everything we do in life, as we work, serve, or worship, should always be our very best effort for our wonderful LORD... <u>and</u> it should be done with JOY!

Match the Nouns and Adjectives!

Team Game: Photocopy two copies of this page or download and print 2 copies from: https://hebrewwithjoy.com/bhj-handouts/ Cut out the pieces. Divide the students into 2 teams and give each team a complete set. The teams turn the pieces face down on a table. On a signal from the leader, teams turn over all of the pieces and try to match each noun with a matching adjective (there are many possible combinations!). First team to match all 12 sets wins the game.
Individual Students: Cut out the pieces, then match the 12 sets and read them.

הַשֵּׁם	הַמֶּלֶךְ	שׁוֹמְרִים
הַקְּהִילָּה	לֵב	קְהִילָּה
הַקְּדוֹשִׁים	הַטּוֹבָה	שֵׁם
שַׁבָּתוֹת	תּוֹרָה	גָּדוֹל
גְּדוֹלִים	הַגָּדוֹל	קָדוֹשׁ
גְּדוֹלָה	הַשַּׁבָּת	הַשּׁוֹמְרִים
גְּדוֹלוֹת	הַגְּדוֹלוֹת	הַגְּדוֹלָה
הַמִּצְוֹת	הַטּוֹב	קְדוֹשָׁה

Lesson 10 Homework

שֵׁם__________

Circle the correct adjective in each phrase, then translate:

1. תּוֹרָה (קָדוֹשׁ, קְדוֹשָׁה, קְדוֹשׁוֹת) ______________________
2. הַמֶּלֶךְ (הַגְּדוֹלָה, גָּדוֹל, הַגָּדוֹל) ______________________
3. שֵׁם (טוֹבִים, טוֹב, הַטּוֹב, טוֹבָה) ______________________
4. לֵבָב (קָדוֹשׁ, קְדוֹשִׁים, הַקָּדוֹשׁ) ______________________
5. הַקְּהִילָּה (טוֹבָה, הַטּוֹב, הַטּוֹבָה) ______________________

6. Translate the following sentences:

A	אַתְּ אוֹהֶבֶת לֵב קָדוֹשׁ.	
B	הִיא נוֹתֶנֶת אֶת תּוֹרָתֶךָ.	
C	הָאָבוֹת שׁוֹמְרִים אֶת הַמִּצְוֹת הַגְּדוֹלוֹת.	
D	אֲנִי זוֹכֵר אֶת הַמּוֹעֲדִים.	
E	הֵם עוֹבְדִים אֶת יְהוָה הַגָּדוֹל.	
F	אֲנַחְנוּ נוֹתְנִים לֶאֱלֹהֵינוּ.	

7. Write three Hebrew words that come from the root ע.ב.ד and their English meanings:

______________ ______________ ______________

______________ ______________ ______________

Throughout the book, you were challenged to memorize a Scripture in Hebrew. .8
Take time right now to practice it until you know it by heart. Then be prepared to recite it in the next lesson (which is also our last lesson!)

English Book and Verse: ________________________________

Hebrew Book and Verse: ________________________________

Lesson 11 – Be Strong

Hebrew prayer when finishing a book of the Torah

Be strong; be strong, and we will be strengthened! חֲזַק חֲזַק וְנִתְחַזֵּק!

2 Samuel 10:12

A – Blessings and Praise in Scripture

Match the following blessings, prayers, and Scriptures to their English translation.

Blessed is the name.		עַם יִשְׂרָאֵל חַי!	1
Morning light.		רְפוּאָה שְׁלֵמָה!	2
Thank you for Israel.		בָּרוּךְ אַתָּה יְהוָה.	3
Blessed are you LORD.		חַג שָׂמֵחַ!	4
Our Father, our King, You are our GOD!		בּוֹקֶר אוֹר!	5
Good morning.		בָּר֣וּךְ הַ֭בָּא בְּשֵׁ֣ם יְהוָ֑ה.	6
To your health!		אָבִינוּ מַלְכֵּנוּ, אַתָּה אֱלֹהֵינוּ!	7
The people of Israel live.		בָּרוּךְ הַשֵּׁם!	8
Joyful holiday!		תּוֹדָה עַל יִשְׂרָאֵל.	9
Blessed are the comers – Welcome!		בּוֹקֶר טוֹב!	10
Complete healing!		לַבְּרִיאוּת!	11
Blessed is the one who comes in the name of the LORD.		בְּרוּכִים הַבָּאִים!	12

B – Reciting Scripture

In previous lessons, you had an opportunity to study one of your favorite Scriptures. Prayerfully, you have successfully memorized it. Take a moment right now to recite it out loud, both in English and in Hebrew. (Share it out loud in your class or with another person.) If this was your first opportunity to memorize a verse in Hebrew, may it be the beginning of many more verses to come!

Today's Date ______________________________

Scripture Reference: ______________________________

C – Final Prayer

You have also had the opportunity to write out your own prayers in Hebrew, GOD's holy language, as a blessing to Him. On the next few lines, write one more prayer to our amazing Father in Hebrew. Be sure to use some of the prayer and Scriptures from this book! Use the dictionaries in the Appendix to help you remember the words from this book or use any other Hebrew resources. Write the prayer in both Hebrew and English.

____ Hebrew

____

____

____

____

____ English

____

____

____

D – Post Quiz

At the beginning of this course, you took a Pre-Quiz to see how much of the course content you already knew. Now is the time to take the Post-Quiz to see much you much you have learned. Please DO NOT use any resources to complete this page.

Match the roots to their meaning: D2			
guard, keep	_____	נ.ת.ן	A
to be wise	_____	שׁ.מ.ר	B
grace, mercy, favor	_____	ד.ב.ר	C
create, shape	_____	ב.ר.א	D
give	_____	צ.ו.ה	E
remember	_____	ז.כ.ר	F
speak, word, thing	_____	ע.ב.ד	G
work, serve, worship	_____	ח.כ.ם	H
command	_____	ח.נ.ן	I

Match the pronouns to their meaning: D1			
I	_____	הֵן	A
you (fs)	_____	אַתְּ	B
they (mpl)	_____	הִיא	C
you (ms)	_____	אַתָּה	D
they (fpl)	_____	אֲנִי	E
he	_____	הֵם	F
she	_____	אֲנַחְנוּ	G
we	_____	הוּא	H

Match the prefixes to their meaning: D3			
to/for	_____	הַ..	A
from	_____	בְּ..	B
in the/with the	_____	לְ..	C
the	_____	וְ..	D
and	_____	מִ..	E
in/with	_____	בַּ..	F

Match the suffixes to their meaning: D4			
me/my	_____	..וֹ	A
you/your	_____	..ךָ	B
his/him	_____	..נוּ	C
our/we	_____	..◌ִי	D

	Translate the sentences into English:	
	בָּרוּךְ בְּנֵי יִשְׂרָאֵל.	D5
	אֲנַחְנוּ נוֹתְנִים לְךָ.	D6
	אֲנִי אוֹהֵב אֶת מִצְוֹתָיו.	D7
	אַתָּה אֱלֹהֵינוּ!	D8

Answers are at the bottom of Appendix B, page 121.

E – Be Strong!

חֲזַק חֲזַק וְנִתְחַזֵּק! E1

Be strong; be strong, and we will be strengthened!

(adapted from 2 Samuel 10:12)

As you have completed the last lesson in *Biblical Hebrew with Joy!*, now is the perfect time to speak the beloved prayer above in **boldness**! You have been strong, you have completed the course, and Adonai will strengthen you to accomplish His will in your life! E2

Please let me know if this book has blessed you and drawn you closer to our amazing LORD. Would you take a moment to post a review on Amazon and/or Google? Or you can email me at hebrewwithjoy33@gmail.com. Todah rabah! E3

If you have taken this course in a class setting, please complete the evaluation on the next page and give it to your teacher. Your מוֹרָה or מוֹרֶה will appreciate the feedback! E4

F – Continuing with Hebrew!

כָּל הַכָּבוֹד! (all the glory/honor!) for successfully completing *Biblical Hebrew with Joy!* F1
בָּרוּךְ הַשֵּׁם! for his Holy Language of עִבְרִית.

Continue to write your personal Hebrew prayers to Adonai. F2

Daily, practice reading the Word of GOD in His holy language, עִבְרִית. F3

The best way to remember what you have learned is to teach someone else! Start right away and take advantage of the free resources that are available on the *Hebrew with Joy!* website. F4

Now I leave you with one of the blessings that you have studied in this course. Can you read it out loud? F5

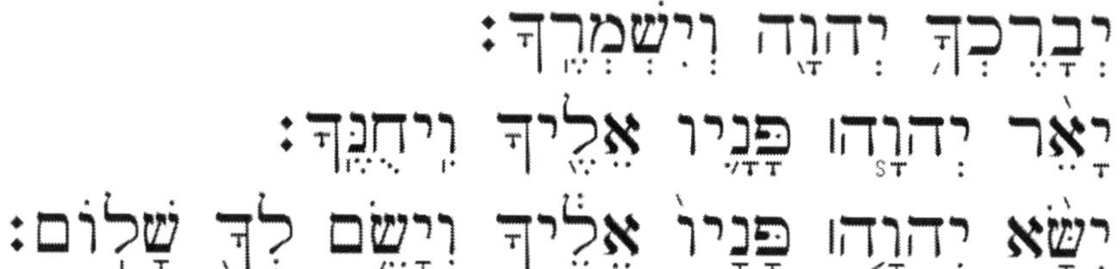

May you be blessed abundantly! My prayers are with you,
Your מוֹרָה,
Joy Carroll

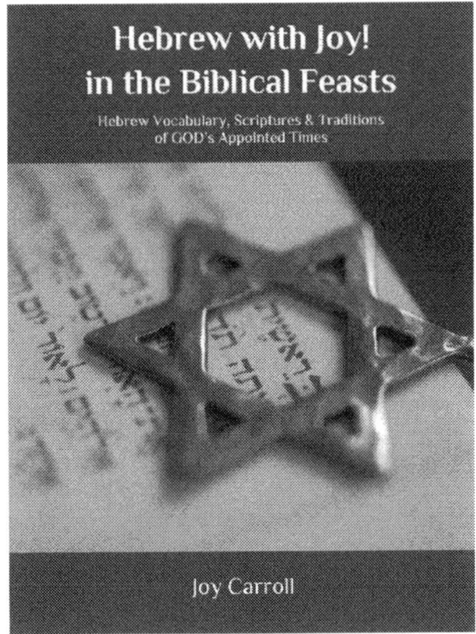

In ***Hebrew with Joy! in the Biblical Feasts***, go deeper in your ability to read Hebrew while learning about GOD's holy "Moadim" – His Appointed Times..

- Examine what the Scriptures say about each Feast and why they are important to the LORD and to us
- Increase your Biblical vocabulary and key roots
- Explore the Israeli traditions for each Feast
- Find helpful suggestions for your own Feast celebrations
- Study with the free Videos, Audios, and PowerPoints included on HebrewWithJoy.com
- Use this book as a yearly resource to prepare for each Feast

Class Evaluation
Biblical Hebrew with Joy!

1. How would you rate this class on a scale of 1 to 5? (5 being the highest) _________
2. What did you like most about the class?
3. What suggestion/s do you have that would make the class better?
4. Would you be willing to write a book review that would encourage others to buy the book? Please post it through Amazon.com (search for: *Biblical Hebrew with Joy!*)

Appendix A - Lesson Fill-Ins

Fill-Ins from right to left!	Line	Lesson
blessed בָּרוּךְ, בֵּרֵךְ, יְבָרֶכְךָ, בְּרָכָה, בְּרָכוֹת	C4-C5	1
יְבָרֶכְךָ	D1	1
LORD, name, blessed	D2	1
יְהוָה, בָּרוּךְ	D3	1
last	B1	2
wisdom, all	D2	2
bread, wind/breath/spirit, king מֶלֶךְ אֱמֶת רוּחַ אֶרֶץ לֶחֶם	D5	2
בָּרוּךְ בְּשֵׁם יִשְׂרָאֵל חָכְמָה עִבְרִית	E5	2
Hebrew, wisdom, Israel, blessed	E5	2
יִשְׂרָאֵל יְבָרֶכְךָ אַהֲבָה וְיִשְׁמְרֶךָ מִתּוֹרָתֶךָ	F4	2
love, Israel	F4	2
wisdom, LORD	H5	2
the earth/land, the heaven/s, the all (everything)	B4	3
wisdom and joy, love and blessings, peace and love	C2	3
in (the), in the land, in a land, in/with joy, in (the) name	D4	3
create/creator	E2	3
amen, the, creator, the, מֶלֶךְ, LORD, בָּרוּךְ	E7	3
God created Abraham, the Lord created Israel	F3	3
the earth, and, the heavens, GOD, created	G2	3
1 בְּרֵאשִׁית בָּרָא אֱלֹהִים אֵת הַשָּׁמַיִם וְאֵת הָאָרֶץ	G5	3
to your health ,to/for joy, to my beloved, to/for Israel	B2	4
to/for, and my beloved, to my beloved, I	B4	4
from your Torah, from Torah, from all, from the LORD	C2	4
guard/keep	D2	4
from all, guard, יְהוָה	D6	4
He guards from Israel/He is a guard from Israel.	E3	4
You are blessed.	E4	4
I guard in Israel/I am a guard in Israel.	E5	4
one, LORD, our God, LORD, Israel, hear	E6	4
Hear, Israel, the LORD our GOD, the LORD is one.	E7	4
hear Israel	G4	4
m-appointed time/season, f-Sabbath, f-blessing m-week, f-commandment	B4	5
f-faith, f-year, m-word/thing, m-day, m-guard	B5	5
sons, appointed times/seasons, words/things, guards, days	C3	5

Overview Pre-Quiz Answers from right to left							
B,C,E,F,A,D	B5	A,C,B,D	B4	G,C,H,E,D,B,F,A	B3	D,C,G,B,H,F,A,E	B2
Blessed are the sons of Israel.	B9	We love his commandments.	B8	You are our God.	B7	He gives to you.	B6

Fill-Ins from right to left!	Line	Lesson
commandments, Sabbaths, blessings	D3	5
m-weeks, m-names, f-years	E2-E4	5
and years, and for days, and for seasons, for, and	E5	5
word/thing	F2	5
words/things, Numbers, names, in the beginning, תְּהִלִּים דְּבָרִים שְׁמוֹת ← circles Psalms, Deuteronomy	G3-G9	5
they love, you love, they love, she loves	B8	6
give/giver	C2	6
אֲנַחְנוּ נוֹתְנִים, הִיא נוֹתֶנֶת, הוּא נוֹתֵן, הֵן נוֹתְנוֹת	C9	6
love, guard, give	D4-D6	6
נוֹתֶנֶת, אוֹהֲבוֹת, שׁוֹמְרִים	D7-D9	6
נוֹתֵן וְנָתַן the Torah, giver, LORD, you, blessed	F2-F3	6
guard of the Torah/instruction, covenant of eternity	B6-B7	7
king of the world/universe	B8	7
day, year, day, life, commandment	B9-12	7
house of bread, God of, sons of Israel	C3	7
congregation of peace, joy of Torah, Joy of the LORD	C5	7
she/it, the LORD, joy (of), Nehemiah	C6	7
commandments, commandment	D2-D3	7
LORD of Peace, Prince of Peace, King of Israel, God of Abraham Creator of Israel, God of the gods, spirit of wisdom	E2-E8	7
to you, your GOD, to you, your Torah/instruction, your peace	B5	8
grace	D5	8
and will keep you, יְהוָה, will bless you, Numbers	E3	8
and will be gracious to you, toward you, his face, יְהוָה	E4	8
peace, to you, and, toward you, his face, יְהוָה	E5	8
to me, my Torah, my name, my Father, my house	B3	9
to my, and light, your word, to my, Psalm	B4	9
to us, we, our Torah, our king, our God, our father	C4	9
the world/universe, מֶלֶךְ, our God, יְהוָה , you, בָּרוּךְ	C5	9
it, his face, his commandments, his Torah, his name, to him	D4	9
to you, his commandments, our king, my name, your Torah	D6	9
your GOD, to him, our GOD, his face, our Torah	D7	9
his name, his Torah, to us, to me, our Father	D8	9
remember	E2	9
holy, to, the Sabbath, day, -, remember, Exodus	E9	9
good guards/guardians, great congregation, holy heart	B7	10
gods, all, great, and king, יְהוָה , great, God, for, Psalm	B8	10
הָאָב הַגָּדוֹל, הַלֵּב הַטּוֹב	B10	10
work/serve/worship	C2	10
LORD, - , serve/worship/work for, and my house, and, Joshua	C7	10
with joy, LORD, -, work/serve/worship, Psalm	C8	10
6,2,12,4,1,11,10,7,3,9,5,8	A1-A12	11

Mid Quiz Answers from right to left

B,D,A,F,E,C	D3	F,H,G,E,D,A,C,B	D2	N,K,F,A,G,B,I,C,H,L,D,J,M,E	D1		
Blessed are the commandments!	D7	We are from Israel.	D6	GOD created the heavens.	D5	You are the king.	D4

Appendix B - Hebrew Phrases

Less	Lesson Phrases		
#	English	Translit.	Hebrew
2	Thanks very much for…	to-DA ra-BA al…	תּוֹדָה רַבָּה עַל...
3	To your health! Get well!	la-bree-OOT	לַבְּרִיאוּת!
4	The people of Israel live!	am yees-ra-EL khai!	עַם יִשְׂרָאֵל חַי!
5	Welcome!/Blessed is the comer (ms) (new baby)	ba-ROOKH ha-BA	בָּרוּךְ הַבָּא!
5	Welcome!/Blessed are the comers (mpl) (newly married)	b-roo-KHEEM ha-ba-EEM	בְּרוּכִים הַבָּאִים!
6	I love you, LORD. (man writing)	a-NEE o-HEV ot-KHA a-do-NAI	אֲנִי אוֹהֵב אוֹתְךָ יְהוָה.
6	I love You, LORD. (woman writing)	a-NEE o-HEV-et ot-KHA a-do-NAI	אֲנִי אוֹהֶבֶת אוֹתְךָ יְהוָה.
7	Holiday of Joy	khag sa-ME-akh	חַג שָׂמֵחַ!
8	Good Morning!	**BO**-ker tov	בֹּקֶר טוֹב!
8	Morning Light!	**BO**-ker or!	בֹּקֶר אוֹר!
9	Our Father, our King, You are our GOD!	a-**VEE**-noo mal-**KE**-noo a-ta e-lo-**HAY**-noo	אָבִינוּ מַלְכֵּנוּ, אַתָּה אֱלֹהֵינוּ!
10	Complete healing!	r-foo-A sh-le-MA	רְפוּאָה שְׁלֵמָה!
11	Be strong, be strong and be strengthened!	kha-ZAK, kha-ZAK, v-neet-kha-ZEK	חֲזַק חֲזַק וְנִתְחַזֵּק

Teacher Classroom Phrases		
English	Translit.	Hebrew
class	kee-TA	כִּיתָּה
correct	na-KHON	נָכוֹן
excellent	me-tsoo-YAN	מְצוּיָּן
finished	**ZE**-o	זֶהוּ
friends		
good	tov	טוֹב
great!/terrific	**YO**-fee	יֹפִי
How are you?	ma-neesh-MA	מַה נִּשְׁמַע?
in Hebrew	b-eev-REET	בְּעִבְרִית
no	lo	לֹא
praise	ha-LEL	הַלֵּל
prayer	t-fee-LA	תְּפִילָּה
quiet!	**SHE**-ket!	שֶׁקֶט!
quiet, please!	**SHE**-ket b-va-ka-SHA!	שֶׁקֶט בְּבַקָּשָׁה!
students	tal-mee-DEEM	תַּלְמִידִים
teacher (fs)	mo-RA	מוֹרָה
teacher (ms)	mo-RE	מוֹרֶה
very good	tov m-OD	טוֹב מְאוֹד
What's this/that?	ma ze?	מַה זֶּה?
yes	ken	כֵּן

Post-Quiz Answers from right to left							
C,A,B,D	D4	B,D,A,F,E,C	D3	E,G,C,F,A,D,I,H,B	D2	G,C,H,A,D,F,B,E	D1
You are our God!	D8	I love his commandments.	D7	We give to you.	D6	Blessed are the sons of Israel.	D5

Appendix C - Hebrew Letters

Sound	Name	Script	Block	Letter
silent	**A**-lef		א	א
b as in **b**ar	Bet (with a dot)		בּ	בּ
v as in **v**ictory	Bet (without a dot)		ב	ב
g as in **g**ap	**GEE**-mel		ג	ג
d as in **d**oor	**DA**-let		ד	ד
h as in **h**oly	Hay		ה	ה
v as in **v**ictory	Vav		ו	ו
z as in **z**eal	**ZA**-yeen		ז	ז
kh as in Ba**ch**	Khet		ח	ח
t as in **t**op	Tet		ט	ט
y as in **y**es	Yood		י	י
k as in **k**ing	Kaf (with a dot)		כּ	כּ
kh as in Ba**ch**	Kaf (without a dot)		כ	כ
kh as in Ba**ch**	Kaf so-FEET		ך	ך
l as in **l**ight	**LA**-med		ל	ל
m as in **m**olehill	Mem		מ	מ
m as in **m**olehill	Mem so-FEET		ם	ם
n as in **n**ame	Noon		נ	נ
n as in **n**ame	Noon so-FEET		ן	ן

Hebrew Letters (cont.)

Sound	Name	Script	Block	Letter
s as in **s**on	**SA**-mekh	ס	ס	ס
silent	**AI**-yeen	ע	ע	ע
p as in **p**ray	Pay (with a dot)	פּ	פּ	פּ
f as in **f**aith	Pay (without a dot)	פ	פ	פ
f as in **f**aith	Pay so-FEET	ף	ף	ף
ts as in roo**ts**	**TSA**-dee	צ	צ	צ
ts as in roo**ts**	**TSA**-dee so-FEET	ץ	ץ	ץ
k as in **k**ing	Koof	ק	ק	ק
r as in **r**est	Raysh	ר	ר	ר
sh as in **sh**ine	Shin	שׁ	שׁ	שׁ
s as in **s**on	Shin	שׂ	שׂ	שׂ
t as in **t**oe	Tav	ת	ת	ת

Appendix D - Hebrew Vowels

Sounds like....	Nee-koo-dot - Vowels		
"a" as in all	◌ָ ka-METZ	◌ֲ kha-TAF pa-TAKH	◌ַ pa-TAKH
"o" as in over (dot is over the letter)	◌ֹ kho-LAM	וֹ kho-LAM ma-LE	
"e" as in egg (3+2=5 eggs in a basket)	◌ֶ se-GOL	◌ֱ kha-TAF se-GOL	◌ֵ TSE-ray
"ee" as in feet (the vowel is under the feet of the letter)	◌ִי KHEE-reek ma-LE	◌ִ KHEE-reek	
silent or **"uh"** as in above (one dot above the other)	◌ְ sh-VA		
"oo" as in too (“ooh- it hurts)	וּ shoo-ROOK	◌ֻ koo-BOOTS	
"akh" as in Bach (exception – at the end of a word)	חַ khet with pa-TAKH		
"ay" as in lay (“e” + “ee”)	◌ֵי TSE-ray Yod		
“ai" as in pie (“a” + “ee”)	◌ַי pa-TAKH yod		
"o" as in flow (exception vowel!)	◌ָ kha-MATZ kha-TOOF		
"oy" as in toy	וֹי kho-LAM ma-LE yod		
"ooey" as in gooey	וּי shoo-ROOK yod		

Appendix E - Roots

Lesson	Meaning	Root
1	love	א.ה.ב
1	bless, kneel	ב.ר.ך
1	live	ח.י.ה
1	hit the mark	י.ר.ה
1	holy	ק.ד.שׁ
1	rest, stop	שׁ.ב.ת
1	completion, wholeness	שׁ.ל.ם
1	joyful	שׂ.מ.ח
1	hear and obey	שׁ.מ.ע
2	to be wise	ח.כ.ם
3	create, shape, form	ב.ר.א
4	guard, keep	שׁ.מ.ר
5	speak, word, thing	ד.ב.ר
6	give	נ.ת.ן
7	command, order	צ.ו.ה
8	grace, mercy, favor	ח.נ.ן
9	remember	ז.כ.ר
10	work, serve, worship	ע.ב.ד

Appendix F – Flashcards

שַׁבָּת	חַיִּים	ב.ר.ך
שָׁלוֹם	קָדוֹשׁ	א.ה.ב
תוֹרָה	שִׂמְחַה	ח.י.ה
שְׁמַע	שׁ.ב.ת	ק.ד.שׁ
בָּרוּךְ	שׁ.ל.ם	יְהוָה יְיָ
אַהֲבָה	י.ר.ה	שֵׁם

bless/kneel root 1	life ms 1	Sabbath fs 1
love root 1	holy ms 1	peace/hello/ goodbye ms 1
live root 1	joy fs 1	instruction fs 1
holy root 1	rest/stop root 1	hear/listen ms 1
Adonai/ LORD 1	completion/ wholeness root 1	blessed ms 1
name ms 1	hit the mark root 1	love fs 1

כָּל	שׂ.מ.ח	שׁ.מ.ע
אֱלֹהִים אֵל	לֶחֶם	יִשְׂרָאֵל
ח.כ.ם	מֶלֶךְ	חָכְמָה
הַ..	אֵת, אֶת	בְּ..
וְ.. וַ.. וָ.. וִ.. וּ..	בַּ..	אֶרֶץ
בּוֹרֵא	שָׁמַיִם	יוֹם

hear/obey root 1	joyful root 1	all 2
Israel fs 2	bread ms 2	God mpl/ms 2
wisdom fs 2	king ms 2	to be wise root 2
in/with prefix 3	specific direct object marker (no translation) 3	the prefix 3
earth/land ms 3	in the/ with the prefix 3	and prefix 3
day ms 3	heaven/s mpl 3	create/ creator ms 3

אַתָּה	אֲנִי	ב.ר.א
שׁוֹמֵר	הוּא	אַתְּ
שׁ.מ.ר	מ..	ל..
דוֹדִי	שָׁבוּעַ	אֲנַחְנוּ, אַנוּ
מוֹעֵד	מִצְוָה	בֵּן
..◌ִים	..וֹת	דָּבָר

create/ shape/form root 3	I ms, fs 4	you ms 4
you fs 4	he/it ms 4	guard/keep ms 4
to/for prefix 4	from prefix 4	guard/keep root 4
we mpl,fpl 5	week ms 5	my beloved ms 4
son/child ms 5	commandment fs 5	appointed time/season ms 5
word/thing ms 5	fpl suffix 5	mpl suffix 5

הֵם	נוֹתֵן	ד.ב.ר
הֵן	נ.ת.ן	הִיא
בְּרִית	עוֹלָם	בַּיִת
חֶדְוָה	קְהִילָּה	צ.ו.ה
לְךָ	אוֹר	חֵן
פָּנָיו	אֵלֶיךָ	לְכֵם

speak/word/thing root 5	give ms 6	they mpl 6
she/it fs 6	give root 6	they fpl 6
house ms 7	forever/eternity world/universe ms 7	covenant fs 7
command root 7	congregation/ community fs 7	joy fs 7
grace ms 8	light/shine ms 8	to you ms 8
to you mpl 8	toward you ms 8	his face ms 8

..ךָ ..כֶם	ח.נ.ן	..י
אֱלֹהֵינוּ	אָב	זוֹכֵר
..נוּ	מִצְוֹתָיו	ז.כ.ר
..◌ִי	..וֹ ..◌ָיו	לֵב/לֵבַב
גָּדוֹל	עוֹבֵד	ע.ב.ד
חֲזַק	כִּי	טוֹב

future action prefix 8	grace/mercy/ favor root 8	you/your suffix ms/mpl 8
remember ms 9	father ms 9	our GOD ms 9
remember root 9	his commandments fpl 9	our/we suffix fpl/mpl 9
heart ms 10	his/him/it suffix ms 10	my/me suffix ms/fs 10
work/serve/ worship root 10	work/serve/ worship ms 10	big/great ms 10
good ms 10	for/because 10	be strong! ms 11

Appendix G - Hebrew Resources

L1 **Book Resources**
Strong's Concordance
Hebrew - English Bible (Interlinear is best)
Hebrew - English Dictionary

L2 **Serve-A-Verse** www.levsoftware.com/SAV/
Free version - choose single verses to hear the Hebrew audio. Paid version has more options including other foreign languages.

L3 **Bible Hub** www.biblehub.com
Free app for phone or computer; includes an interlinear option where you can see the Hebrew text with vowels, English word-for-word translation and Strong's concordance.

L4 **iTranslate** www.itranslate.com
Free app that translates English to Hebrew for iPhone or iPad includes Hebrew voice translation.

L4 **Google Translate** translate.google.com
Free app for phone or computer.

L5 **Blue Letter Bible** www.blueletterbible.org
Free app for phone or computer; has user friendly verse look-up with large easy-to-read Hebrew interlinear (includes vowels!)

L6 **Pealim** www.pealim.com
Free computer version, paid cell phone app. Pealim (meaning verbs) allows you to enter an English or Hebrew word to see all the verb forms.

L7 **Prolog Hebrew-English Dictionary** learnhebrew.prolog.co.il
Free app for phone or computer - there is a one time charge for the complete dictionary which includes vowels, accents and genders.

L9 **Bible Gateway** biblegateway.com
Free Bible program for phone or computer; search for specific Scriptures to see Hebrew translations side-by-side next to the English!
A Westminster Leningrad Codex (WLC) for the Tanakh (Old Testament)
B HaBrit HaKhadasha/HaDereck (HHH) for the Brit Khadashah (New Testament)

Appendix H - Complete Prefix List

Example	Meaning	Prefix
הַמֶּלֶךְ	the	הַ..
וְשָׁמַיִם	and	ו.. וּ..
לְיִשְׂרָאֵל	to/for	ל..
בְּבַיִת	in/with	בְּ.. ב..
בַּבַּיִת	in the/with the	בַּ..
מִיִּשְׂרָאֵל	from	מ..
כֵּאלֹהֵינוּ	like/as	כּ..
שֶׁשּׁוֹמֵר	that/which/who	שׁ..

Appendix I - Complete Suffix List

Example	Meaning	Suffix
אַהֲבָה	feminine singular word	ה ת
בְּרָכוֹת	feminine plural suffix	..וֹת
מוֹעֲדִים	masculine plural suffix	..◌ִים
בְּנֵי יִשְׂרָאֵל	masculine plural word pair suffix	..◌ֵי
קְהִילַּת עֵץ חַיִּים	feminine singular word pair suffix	..◌ַת
תּוֹרָתְךָ	you/your (ms)	..ךָ
שְׁלוֹמֵךְ	you/your (fs)	..ךְ
בֵּיתְכֶם	you/your (mpl)	..כֶם
בֵּיתְכֶן	you/your (fpl)	..כֶן
אֱלֹהֵינוּ	our/we	..נוּ
אָבִי	my/me	..◌ַי ..◌ִי
מִצְוֹתָיו שְׁמוֹ	his/him/it	..וֹ, ..יו
בֵּיתָהּ	her/she/it	..◌ָהּ
תּוֹרָתֶהֶם	their (mpl)	..ֶהֶם, ..ם
תּוֹרָתֶהֶן	their (fpl)	..ֶהֶן, ..ן

Appendix J - Complete Pronoun List

English	Hebrew
I	אֲנִי, אָנֹכִי
you (ms)	אַתָּה
you (fs)	אַתְּ
he, it	הוּא
she, it	הִיא
we	אֲנַחְנוּ, אָנוּ
you (mpl)	אַתֶּם
you (fpl)	אַתֶּן
they (mpl)	הֵם, הֵמָּה
they (fpl)	הֵן, הֵנָּה

Appendix K – Tanakh Book Names

English Name	Hebrew	Transliteration
1st Chronicles	דִּבְרֵי הַיָּמִים א	deev-RAY ha-ya-MEEM A-lef
2nd Chronicles	דִּבְרֵי הַיָּמִים ב	deev-RAY ha-ya-MEEM bet
Amos	עָמוֹס	a-MOS
Daniel	דָּנִיֵּאל	da-nee-YEL
Deuteronomy	דְּבָרִים	d-va-REEM
Ecclesiastes	קֹהֶלֶת	ko-**HE**-let
Esther	אֶסְתֵּר	es-TER
Exodus	שְׁמוֹת	sh-MOT
Ezekiel	יְחֶזְקֵאל	y-khez-KEL
Ezra	עֶזְרָא	ez-RA
Genesis	בְּרֵאשִׁית	b-re-SHEET
Habakkuk	חֲבַקּוּק	kha-va-KOOK
Haggai	חַגַּי	kha-GAI
Hosea	הוֹשֵׁעַ	ho-**SHAY**-a
Isaiah	יְשַׁעְיָהוּ	y-sha-**YA**-hoo
Jeremiah	יִרְמְיָהוּ	yeer-m-**YA**-hoo
Job	אִיּוֹב	ee-OV
Joel	יוֹאֵל	yo-EL
Jonah	יוֹנָה	yo-NA
Joshua	יְהוֹשֻׁעַ	y-**HO**-shoo-a
Judges	שׁוֹפְטִים	shof-TEEM
Kings	מְלָכִים	m-la-KHEEM
Lamentations	אֵיכָה	ay-KHA
Leviticus	וַיִּקְרָא	va-yeek-RA
Malachi	מַלְאָכִי	mal-a-KHEE
Micah	מִיכָה	mee-KHA

Appendix K – Tanakh Book Names

English Name	Hebrew	Transliteration
Nahum	נַחוּם	na-KHUM
Nehemiah	נְחֶמְיָה	n-khem-YA
Numbers	בַּמִּדְבָּר	ba-meed-BAR
Obadiah	עֹבַדְיָה	o-vad-YA
Proverbs	מִשְׁלֵי	meesh-LAY
Psalms	תְּהִלִּים	t-hee-LEEM
Ruth	רוּת	root
Samuel	שְׁמוּאֵל	shmoo-EL
Song of Songs	שִׁיר הַשִּׁירִים	sheer ha-shee-REEM
Zechariah	זְכַרְיָה	z-khar-YA
Zephaniah	צְפַנְיָה	ts-fan-YA

Appendix L - Torah Treasures Index

Scriptural and Cultural Treasures	Line	Lesson
Blessed are You Adonai	D4	1
Blessed is the Name	E2	1
Pronouncing Biblical Names	B3	2
Bread	D6	2
Hebrew	E6	2
Memorizing Scripture	G3	2
Ancient Wisdom	H6	2
Vav, the Tabernacle and the Torah	C3	3
Word Order – Biblical vs. Modern	G4	3
To Life	B3	4
Ketubah	B5	4
Elul	B7	4
Sh'ma	E8	4
Where are the Vowels?	G4	4
Faith, Truth and Amen	B6	5
Majestic Plurals	C4	5
In the Wilderness	F7	5
Tanakh	G1	5
Parasha	F1	6
Sabbath Peace	B5	7
Rosh Hashana Vs Yom T'ruah	B14	7
Meditate on Adonai	E1	7
Blessing of the Priests	E1	8
Hannah Nesher Aaronic Blessing	F1	8
Priestly Hands	F2	8
Psalm 119:105	B5	9
Ancient Father	C6	9
Remember	E10	9
Tov	A6	10
Hebrew Adjectives	B11	10
Psalm 100:2	C9	10

Appendix M - Hebrew Prayers

Kiddush (Sanctification) - Blessing over the Wine

בָּרוּךְ אַתָּה יְהוָה אֱלֹהֵינוּ מֶלֶךְ הָעוֹלָם בּוֹרֵא פְּרִי הַגָּפֶן. אָמֵן.

ba-ROOKH a-TA a-do-NAI, e-lo-**HAY**-noo **ME**-lekh ha-o-LAM, bo-RE p-REE ha-**GA**-fen. *a-MEN*

Blessed are you, Adonai, our God, Ruler of the universe, Creator of the fruit of the vine. Amen

HaMotsee (Who Brings Forth) - Blessing over the Bread

בָּרוּךְ אַתָּה יְהוָה אֱלֹהֵינוּ מֶלֶךְ הָעוֹלָם הַמּוֹצִיא לֶחֶם מִן הָאָרֶץ. אָמֵן

ba-ROOKH a-TA a-do-NAI, e-lo-**HAY**-noo **ME**-lekh ha-o-LAM, ha-**MO**-tsee **LE**-khem meen ha-**A**-rets. a-MEN

Blessed are You, Adonai our God, Ruler of the universe, who brings forth bread from the earth. Amen

Sh'ma

שְׁמַע יִשְׂרָאֵל יְהוָה אֱלֹהֵינוּ יְהוָה אֶחָד׃
בָּרוּךְ שֵׁם כְּבוֹד מַלְכוּתוֹ לְעוֹלָם וָעֶד׃

sh-MA yees-ra-EL a-do-NAI e-lo-**HAY**-noo a-do-NAI e-KHAD:
ba-ROOKH shem k-VOD mal-**KHOO**-to l-o-LAM va-ED.

Hear (O) Israel, The LORD our God, the LORD is one.
Blessed is the name of His glorious kingdom for ever and ever.

The Aaronic Blessing:

יְבָרֶכְךָ יְהוָה וְיִשְׁמְרֶךָ׃ יָאֵר יְהוָה פָּנָיו אֵלֶיךָ וִיחֻנֶּךָּ׃
יִשָּׂא יְהוָה פָּנָיו אֵלֶיךָ וְיָשֵׂם לְךָ שָׁלוֹם׃

y-va-**RE**-kh-kha a-do-NAI v-yeesh-m-**RE**-kha; ya-ER a-do-NAI pa-NAV e-**LE**-kha vee-khoo-**NE**-kha;
yee-SA a-do-NAI pa-NAV e-**LE**-kha v-ya-SEM l-KHA sha-LOM

Adonai bless you and keep you! Adonai make His face to shine on you and be gracious to you!
Adonai turn his face to you and grant you shalom. Numbers 6:24-26

Appendix N – Hebrew- English Dictionary 1

Lesson #	English	Gender	Transliteration	Hebrew
9	his/him suffix	*ms, mpl*	..o ..av	..וֹ ..◌ָיו
7	you/your suffix	*ms*	...kha	..ךָ
7	you/your suffix	*mpl*	...khem	..כֶם
9	our/we suffix	*mpl*	..noo	..נוּ
5	feminine plural suffix	*fpl*	..ot	..וֹת
5	masculine plural suffix	*mpl*	..eem	..◌ִים
1	love	*root*	-	א.ה.ב
9	father	*ms*	av	אָב
7	Abraham	*ms*	av-ra-HAM	אַבְרָהָם
1	love - noun	*fs*	a-ha-VA	אַהֲבָה
6	love - verb	*ms*	o-HEV	אוֹהֵב
8	light/shine	*ms*	or	אוֹר
6	you (direct object)	*ms*	ot-KHA	אוֹתְךָ
6	you (direct object)	*fs*	o-TAKH	אוֹתָךְ
4	one	*ms*	e-KHAD	אֶחָד
2	God	*ms* *mpl*	el e-lo-HEEM	אֵל, אֱלֹהִים
7	God of	*mpl*	e-lo-HAI	אֱלֹהֵי
9	our God	*mpl*	e-lo-**HAY**-noo	אֱלֹהֵינוּ
8	toward you/upon you	*ms*	e-**LE**-kha	אֵלֶיךָ
5	faith	*fs*	e-moo-NA	אֱמוּנָה
2	truth	*fs*	**E**-met	אֱמֶת
5	we	*mpl/fpl*	a-**NAKH**-noo, **A**-noo	אֲנַחְנוּ, אַנוּ
4	I	*ms, fs*	a-NEE	אֲנִי
2	earth/land	*ms*	**E**-retz	אֶרֶץ
4	you	*fs*	at	אַתְּ
3	specific direct object marker	-	et	אֵת, אֶת
4	you	*ms*	a-TA	אַתָּה
3	in/with in the/with the	*prefix*	b... ba..	..בְּ ..בַּ
3	create, shape, form	*root*	-	ב.ר.א
1	bless, kneel	*root*	-	ב.ר.ך
4	morning	*ms*	**BO**-ker	בּוֹקֶר

Appendix N – Hebrew- English Dictionary 2

Lesson #	English	Gender	Transliteration	Hebrew
3	create/creator	*ms*	bo-RE	בּוֹרֵא
7	house of	*ms*	bayt	בֵּית
7	house	*ms*	**BA**-yeet	בַּיִת
5	in the desert (book of Numbers)	*ms*	ba-meed-BAR	בַּמִּדְבָּר
5	son/child	*ms*	ben	בֵּן
7	sons of	*mpl*	b-NAY	בְּנֵי
5	son	*ms*	bar (Aramaic)	בַּר
3	created	*ms*	ba-RA	בָּרָא
3	beginning	*ms*	b-re-SHEET	בְּרֵאשִׁית
5	Genesis	*ms*	b-re-SHEET	בְּרֵאשִׁית
1	blessed	*ms*	ba-ROOKH	בָּרוּךְ
3	health	*ms*	b-ree-OOT	בְּרִיאוּת
7	covenant	*fs*	b-REET	בְּרִית
1	knee	*fs*	**BE**-rekh	בֶּרֶךְ
1	blessing	*fs*	b-ra-KHA	בְּרָכָה
2	in the name	*ms*	b-SHEM	בְּשֵׁם
7	daughter	*fs*	bat	בַּת
10	big/great	*adj*	ga-DOL	גָּדוֹל
5	speak, word, thing	*root*	-	ד.ב.ר
5	word/thing	*ms*	da-VAR	דָּבָר
5	words	*mpl*	d-va-REEM	דְּבָרִים
5	Deuteronomy	*mpl*	d-va-REEM	דְּבָרִים
4	my beloved, (my uncle!)	*ms*	do-DEE	דוֹדִי
3	the	*prefix*	ha	הַ..
2	land/earth, the	*fs*	ha-**A**-rets	הָאָרֶץ
1	the one who comes	*ms*	ha-BA	הַבָּא
4	he/it	*ms*	hoo	הוּא
6	she/it	*fs*	hee	הִיא
3	today	*ms*	ha-YOM	הַיּוֹם
2	everything	*adj*	ha-KOL	הַכָּל
6	they	*mpl* *fpl*	hem hen	הֵם הֵן

Appendix N – Hebrew- English Dictionary 3

Lesson #	English	Gender	Transliteration	Hebrew
1	the name	mpl	ha-SHEM	הַשֵּׁם
3	and	prefix	v.. oo..	וְ.. וּ..
5	Leviticus, book of	ms	va-yeek-RA	וַיִּקְרָא
9	remember	root	-	ז.כ.ר
9	remember	ms	zo-KHER	זוֹכֵר
1	live	root	-	ח.י.ה
2	to be wise	root	-	ח.כ.ם
8	grace	root	-	ח.נ.ן
7	joyful holiday	ms	khag sa-**ME**-akh	חַג שָׂמֵחַ!
7	joy (belonging to GOD)	fs	khed-VA	חֶדְוָה
11	be strong!	ms	kha-ZAK	חֲזַק
1	life	mpl	khai-YEEM	חַיִּים
2	wise	ms	kha-KHAM	חָכָם
2	wisdom	fs	khokh-MA (exception vowel)	חָכְמָה
8	grace	ms	khen	חֵן
10	good	adj	tov	טוֹב
9	my/me	suffix	ee	..ִי
1	hit the mark	root	-	י.ר.ה
1	LORD	-	a-do-NAI, ha-SHEM ye-ho-VA, ya	יְהוָה
3	day	ms	yom	יוֹם
6	Jonathan (GOD gave)	ms	yo-na-TAN	יוֹנָתָן
2	Israel	fs	yees-ra-EL	יִשְׂרָאֵל
11	honor/glory	ms	ka-VOD	כָּבוֹד
10	for/because	-	kee	כִּי
2	all	adj	kol (exception)	כָּל
7	atonement	ms	kee-POOR	כִּפּוּר
4	marriage contract	fs	k-too-BA	כְּתֻבָּה
5	writings	mpl	k-too-VEEM	כְּתוּבִים
4	to/for	prefix	L..	לְ..
10	heart	ms	lev, le-VAV	לֵב/לֵבָב
3	to (your) health! (get well)	fpl	la-b-ree-OOT	לַבְּרִיאוּת!
4	to life	mpl	l-khai-YEEM	לְחַיִּים

Appendix N – Hebrew- English Dictionary 4

Lesson #	English	Gender	Transliteration	Hebrew
2	bread	*ms*	**LE**-khem	לֶחֶם
8	to you	*ms*	l-KHA	לְךָ
8	to you	*mpl*	l-KHEM	לָכֶם
4	from	*prefix*	m..	מ..
5	speak/talk	*ms*	m-da-BER	מְדַבֵּר
5	appointed time/season	*ms*	mo-ED	מוֹעֵד
2	king	*ms*	**ME**-lekh	מֶלֶךְ
5	commandment	*fs*	meets-VA	מִצְוָה
9	his commandments	*fpl*	meets-vo-TAV	מִצְוֹתָיו
5	Proverbs, book of	*ms*	meesh-LAY	מִשְׁלֵי
6	gift	*fs*	ma-ta-NA	מַתָּנָה
6	give	*root*	-	נ.ת.ן
5	prophets	*mpl*	n-vee-EEM	נְבִיאִים
6	give	*ms*	no-TEN	נוֹתֵן
2	joyful cry	*fs*	n-ra-n-NA	נְרַנְּנָה
10	work, serve, worship	*root*	-	ע.ב.ד
10	slave	*ms*	**E**-ved	עֶבֶד
10	Obadiah (servant of God)	*ms*	o-vad-YA	עֹבַדְיָה
10	work/serve/worship	*ms-noun*	a-vo-DA	עֲבוֹדָה
2	Hebrew	*fs*	eev-REET	עִבְרִית
10	work/serve/worship	*ms -verb*	o-VED	עוֹבֵד
7	forever/eternity/world/ universe	*ms*	o-LAM	עוֹלָם
7	tree	*ms*	ets	עֵץ
2	evening	*ms*	**E**-rev	עֶרֶב
5	10 Words (10 Commandments)	*mpl*	a-**SE**-ret ha-d-va-REEM	עֲשֶׂרֶת הַדְּבָרִים
8	his face	*mpl*	pa-NAV	פָּנָיו
9	face	*ms*	pa-NEEM	פָּנִים
6	Torah portion	*fs*	pa-ra-SHA	פָּרָשָׁה
7	command	*root*	-	צ.ו.ה
1	holy	*root*	-	ק.ד.ש

Appendix N – Hebrew- English Dictionary 5

Lesson #	English	Gender	Transliteration	Hebrew
1	holy	*ms*	ka-DOSH	קָדוֹשׁ
7	community/congregation	*fs*	k-hee-LA	קְהִילָּה
7	head	*ms*	rosh	רֹאשׁ
2	much, many, a lot	*adj*	ra-BA	רַבָּה
6	spirit/breath/wind	*fs*	**ROO**-akh	רוּחַ
10	complete healing	*fs*	r-foo-A sh-le-MA	רְפוּאָה שְׁלֵמָה
1	rest, stop	*root*	-	שׁ.ב.ת
1	completion wholeness	*root*	-	שׁ.ל.ם
1	joyful	*root*	-	שׂ.מ.ח
1	hear and obey	*root*	-	ע.מ.שׁ
4	guard, keep	*root*	-	שׁ.מ.ר
5	week	*fs*	sha-**VOO**-a	שָׁבוּעַ
1	Sabbath	*fs*	sha-BAT	שַׁבָּת
4	guard/keep	*ms*	sho-MER	שׁוֹמֵר
1	peace/hello/goodbye	*ms*	sha-LOM	שָׁלוֹם
5	name	*ms*	shem	שֵׁם
5	Exodus, book of	*fpl*	sh-MOT	שְׁמוֹת
1	joy	*fs*	seem-KHA	שִׂמְחָה
3	heaven/s	*mpl*	sha-MAI-yeem	שָׁמַיִם
1	hear/listen	*ms*	sh-MA	שְׁמַע
5	year	*fs*	sha-NA	שָׁנָה
7	prince	*ms*	sar	שַׂר
5	Psalms, book of	*mpl*	t-hee-LEEM	תְּהִלִּים
2	thanks	*ms*	to-DA	תּוֹדָה
1	instruction	*fs*	to-RAH	תּוֹרָה
5	Tanakh	*ms*	ta-NAKH	תָּנָ״ךְ
9	prayer	*fs*	t-fee-LA	תְּפִילָּה
7	blasting	*fs*	t-roo-A	תְּרוּעָה

Appendix O - English-Hebrew Dictionary 1

Lesson #	English	Gender	Transliteration	Hebrew
5	10 Words (10 Commandments)	*mpl*	a-**SE**-ret ha-d-va-REEM	עֲשֶׂרֶת הַדְּבָרִים
7	Abraham	*ms*	av-ra-HAM	אַבְרָהָם
2	All	*adj*	kol (exception)	כָּל
3	And	*prefix*	v... oo..	וְ.. וּ..
5	appointed time/season	*ms*	mo-ED	מוֹעֵד
7	atonement	*ms*	kee-POOR	כִּפּוּר
11	be strong!	*ms*	kha-ZAK	חֲזַק
3	beginning	*ms*	b-re-SHEET	בְּרֵאשִׁית
10	big/great	*adj*	ga-DOL	גָּדוֹל
7	Blasting	*fs*	t-roo-A	תְּרוּעָה
1	bless, kneel	*root*	-	ב.ר.ךְ
1	Blessed	*ms*	ba-ROOKH	בָּרוּךְ
1	Blessing	*fs*	b-ra-KHA	בְּרָכָה
2	Bread	*ms*	**LE**-khem	לֶחֶם
7	command	*root*	-	צ.ו.ה
5	commandment	*fs*	meets-VA	מִצְוָה
7	community/congregation	*fs*	k-hee-LA	קְהִילָּה
10	complete healing	*fs*	r-foo-A sh-le-MA	רְפוּאָה שְׁלֵמָה
1	completion wholeness	*root*	-	שׁ.ל.ם
7	covenant	*fs*	b-REET	בְּרִית
3	create, shape, form	*root*	-	ב.ר.א
3	create/creator	*ms*	bo-RE	בּוֹרֵא
3	Created	*ms*	ba-RA	בָּרָא
7	daughter	*fs*	bat	בַּת
3	Day	*ms*	yom	יוֹם
5	Deuteronomy, book of	*mpl*	d-va-REEM	דְּבָרִים
2	earth/land	*ms*	**E**-retz	אֶרֶץ
2	Evening	*ms*	**E**-rev	עֶרֶב
2	everything	*adj*	ha-KOL	הַכֹּל
5	Exodus, book of	*fpl*	sh-MOT	שְׁמוֹת
9	Face	*ms*	pa-NEEM	פָּנִים
5	Faith	*fs*	e-moo-NA	אֱמוּנָה
9	Father	*ms*	av	אָב
5	feminine plural suffix	*fpl*	ot	..וֹת

Appendix O - English-Hebrew Dictionary - 2

Lesson #	English	Gender	Transliteration	Hebrew
10	for/because	-	kee	כִּי
7	forever/eternity/world/ universe	*ms*	o-LAM	עוֹלָם
4	From	*prefix*	m..	מ..
5	Genesis, book of	*ms*	b-re-SHEET	בְּרֵאשִׁית
6	Gift	*fs*	ma-ta-NA	מַתָּנָה
6	Give	*root*	-	נ.ת.ן
6	Give	*ms*	no-TEN	נוֹתֵן
2	God	*ms* *mpl*	el e-lo-HEEM	אֵל, אֱלֹהִים
7	God of	*mpl*	e-lo-HAI	אֱלֹהֵי
10	Good	*adj*	tov	טוֹב
8	Grace	*root*	-	ח.נ.ן
8	Grace	*ms*	khen	חֵן
4	guard, keep	*root*	-	שׁ.מ.ר
4	guard/keep	*ms*	sho-MER	שׁוֹמֵר
4	he/it	*ms*	hoo	הוּא
7	Head	*ms*	rosh	רֹאשׁ
3	Health	*ms*	b-ree-OOT	בְּרִיאוּת
1	hear/listen	*ms*	sh-MA	שְׁמַע
1	hear and obey	*root*	-	שׁ.מ.ע
10	heart	*ms*	lev, le-VAV	לֵב/לֵבַב
3	heaven/s	*mpl*	sha-MAI-yeem	שָׁמַיִם
2	Hebrew	*fs*	eev-REET	עִבְרִית
9	his commandments	*fpl*	meets-vo-TAV	מִצְוֹתָיו
8	his face	*mpl*	pa-NAV	פָּנָיו
9	his/him	*suffix*	..o ..av	..וֹ ..◌ָיו
1	hit the mark	*root*	-	י.ר.ה
1	Holy	*root*	-	ק.ד.שׁ
1	Holy	*ms*	ka-DOSH	קָדוֹשׁ
11	honor/glory	*ms*	ka-VOD	כָּבוֹד
7	house	*ms*	**BA**-yeet	בַּיִת
7	house of	*ms*	bayt	בֵּית
4	I	*ms, fs*	a-NEE	אֲנִי

Appendix O - English-Hebrew Dictionary - 3

Lesson #	English	Gender	Transliteration	Hebrew
5	in the desert (book of Numbers)	*ms*	ba-meed-BAR	בַּמִּדְבָּר
2	in the name	*ms*	b-SHEM	בְּשֵׁם
3	in/with in the/with the	*prefix*	b... ba..	..בְּ ..בַּ
1	instruction	*fs*	to-RAH	תּוֹרָה
2	Israel	*fs*	yees-ra-EL	יִשְׂרָאֵל
6	Jonathan (GOD gave)	*ms*	yo-na-TAN	יוֹנָתָן
7	joy (belonging to GOD)	*fs*	khed-VA	חֶדְוָה
1	joy	*fs*	seem-KHA	שִׂמְחָה
1	joyful	*root*	-	ש.מ.ח
2	joyful cry	*fs*	n-ra-n-NA	נְרַנְּנָה
7	joyful holiday	*ms*	khag sa-**ME**-akh	חַג שָׂמֵחַ!
2	king	*ms*	**ME**-lekh	מֶלֶךְ
1	knee	*fs*	**BE**-rekh	בֶּרֶךְ
2	land/earth, the	*fs*	ha-**E**-rets	הָאָרֶץ
5	Leviticus, book of	*ms*	va-yeek-RA	וַיִּקְרָא
1	life	*mpl*	khai-YEEM	חַיִּים
8	light/shine	*ms*	or	אוֹר
1	live	*root*	-	ח.י.ה
1	LORD	-	a-do-NAI, ye-ho-VA ha-SHEM, ya	יְהוָה
1	love	*root*	-	א.ה.ב
1	love - noun	*fs*	a-ha-VA	אַהֲבָה
6	love - verb	*ms*	o-HEV	אוֹהֵב
4	marriage contract	*fs*	k-too-BA	כְּתֻבָּה
5	masculine plural suffix	*suffix*	eem	..◌ִים
4	morning	*ms*	**BO**-ker	בּוֹקֶר
2	much, many a lot	*adj*	ra-BA	רַבָּה
4	my beloved, (my uncle!)	*ms*	do-DEE	דּוֹדִי
9	my/me	*suffix*	ee	..◌ִי
5	name	*ms*	shem	שֵׁם

Appendix O - English-Hebrew Dictionary 4

Lesson #	English	Gender	Transliteration	Hebrew
5	Numbers, book of	*ms*	ba-meed-BAR	בַּמִּדְבָּר
10	Obadiah (servant of God)	*ms*	o-vad-YA	עֹבַדְיָה
4	one	*ms*	e-KHAD	אֶחָד
9	our God	*mpl*	e-lo-**HAY**-noo	אֱלֹהֵינוּ
9	our/we	*suffix*	noo	..נוּ
1	peace/hello/goodbye	*ms*	sha-LOM	שָׁלוֹם
9	prayer	*fs*	t-fee-LA	תְּפִילָה
7	prince	*ms*	sar	שַׂר
5	prophets	*mpl*	n-vee-EEM	נְבִיאִים
5	Proverbs, book of	*ms*	meesh-LAY	מִשְׁלֵי
5	Psalms, book of	*mpl*	t-hee-LEEM	תְּהִלִּים
9	remember	*root*	-	ז.כ.ר
9	remember	*ms*	zo-KHER	זוֹכֵר
1	rest, stop	*root*	-	שׁ.ב.ת
1	Sabbath	*fs*	sha-BAT	שַׁבָּת
6	she/it	*fs*	hee	הִיא
10	slave	*ms*	**E**-ved	עֶבֶד
5	son/child	*ms*	ben	בֵּן
5	son	*ms*	bar (Aramaic)	בַּר
7	sons of	*mpl*	b-NAY	בְּנֵי
5	speak, word, thing	*root*	-	ד.ב.ר
5	speak/talk	*ms*	m-da-BER	מְדַבֵּר
3	specific direct object marker	-	et	אֵת, אֶת
6	spirit/breath/wind	*fs*	**ROO**-akh	רוּחַ
5	Tanakh	*ms*	ta-NAKH	תָּנָ"ךְ
2	thanks	*ms*	to-DA	תּוֹדָה
3	the	*prefix*	ha	..הַ
1	the name	*mpl*	ha-SHEM	הַשֵּׁם
1	the one who comes	*ms*	ha-BA	הַבָּא
6	they	*mpl* *fpl*	hem hen	הֵם הֵן

Appendix O - English-Hebrew Dictionary 5

Lesson #	English	Gender	Transliteration	Hebrew
3	To (your) health! (get well)	*fpl*	la-b-ree-OOT	לַבְּרִיאוּת!
2	to be wise	*root*	-	ח.כ.ם
4	to life	*mpl*	l-khai-YEEM	לְחַיִּים
8	to you	*ms*	l-KHA	לְךָ
8	to you	*mpl*	l-KHEM	לְכֶם
4	to/for	*prefix*	l…	לְ..
3	today	*ms*	ha-YOM	הַיּוֹם
6	Torah portion	*fs*	pa-ra-SHA	פָּרָשָׁה
8	toward you/upon you	*ms*	e-**LE**-kha	אֵלֶיךָ
7	tree	*ms*	ets	עֵץ
2	truth	*fs*	**E**-met	אֱמֶת
5	we	*mpl/fpl*	a-**NAKH**-noo, **A**-noo	אֲנַחְנוּ, אֲנוּ
5	week	*fs*	sha-**VOO**-a	שָׁבוּעַ
2	wind, breath, spirit	*ms*	**ROO**-akh	רוּחַ
2	wisdom	*fs*	khokh-MA (exception vowel)	חָכְמָה
2	wise	*ms*	kha-KHAM	חָכָם
5	word/thing	*ms*	da-VAR	דָּבָר
5	words	*mpl*	d-va-REEM	דְּבָרִים
10	work, serve, worship	*root*	-	ע.ב.ד
10	work/serve/worship	*ms - noun*	a-vo-DA	עֲבוֹדָה
10	work/serve/worship	*ms - verb*	o-VED	עוֹבֵד
5	writings	*mpl*	k-too-VEEM	כְּתוּבִים
5	year	*fs*	sha-NA	שָׁנָה
4	you	*fs*	at	אַתְּ
4	you	*ms*	a-TA	אַתָּה
6	you (direct object)	*ms*	ot-KHA	אוֹתְךָ
6	you (direct object)	*fs*	o-TAKH	אוֹתָךְ
7	you/your	*suffix ms*	…kha	..ךָ
7	you/your	*suffix mpl*	…khem	..כֶם

Made in the USA
Columbia, SC
28 October 2024

45053571R00087